TOTAL STEWARDSHIP

A STEP-BY-STEP GUIDE TO MASTERING PERSONAL & CHURCH FINANCES

CRAIG A. DUNN
LARRY MOORE
STAN TOLER

Copyright © 2015 by Craig A. Dunn, Larry Moore and Stan Toler

©2015 Published by Wesleyan Investment Foundation
*Total Stewardship: A Step-by-Step Guide to Mastering Personal & Church Finances/
Craig A. Dunn, Larry Moore and Stan Toler*

Printed in the United States of America

ISBN: 978-1-943140-44-2

All Scripture quotations, unless otherwise indicated, are taken from the Holy Bible, New International Version®, NIV ®. Copyright ©1973, 1978, 1984, 2011 by Biblica, Inc. Used by permission of Zondervan. All rights reserved worldwide. www.zondervan.com. The "NIV" and "New International Version" are trademarks registered in the United States Patent and Trademark Office by Biblica, Inc.

Scripture quotations marked (NLT) are taken from the Holy Bible, New Living Translation, copyright © 1996, 2004, 2007 by Tyndale House Foundation. Used by permission of Tyndale House Publishers, Inc., Carol Stream, Illinois 60188. All rights reserved.

Cover and Interior Design by D.E. West, Dust Jacket Creative Services

WESLEYAN INVESTMENT FOUNDATION

CONTENTS

Introduction v

Part 1: WHOLE LIFE STEWARDSHIP
Seven Things You Must Know
to Experience God's Blessing 1
1. Six Key Principles You Must Understand about Money 3
2. The Essential Difference between Ownership and Stewardship 9
3. The Prosperity Trap 15
4. The Hidden Value of Time 19
5. How to Maximize Your Talents 25
6. Three Steps to Creating Financial Impact 29
7. The One Thing Generous People Know 33

Part 2: PERSONAL FINANCES
Your Ten Step Roadmap to Financial Freedom 37
8. Developing a Financial Roadmap 39
9. The How and Why of Retirement Planning 45
10. You Need an Estate Plan! 51

Part 3: CHURCH FINANCES
Benchmarks for Healthy Churches 55
11. The ABC's of the Pastor's Pay 57
12. Church Budgeting Made Easy 61
13. Accountability: Your Stay Out of Jail Free Card 67
14. How to Create a Financial Dashboard 71
15. The Six Most Common Errors in Handling Charitable Gifts 75

Part 4: FUND DEVELOPMENT
   What Could You Do with More Money? 79
16. How to Create New Givers 81
17. The Most Common Mistake in Capital Fund Drives 85
18. Twelve Steps to a Successful Campaign 89
19. How to Talk to a Banker: What You Need to Secure a Loan 97
20. Six Types of Money You're Leaving on the Table 101

Afterword..**105**
Appendix **107**

INTRODUCTION

This book describes a completely new way of understanding stewardship than most of us are used to. Simply put, it begins with a lifestyle of abundance, generosity, and openness to others, and it leads to our open-handed management of all that God has given to us. When we recognize two foundational truths, everything else falls into line.

Truth One: God has blessed us abundantly with all that we need in this world.

Truth Two: God invites us to join him in tending to the good world he created.

When you understand that, you understand everything. These two ideas will change the way you think about stewardship. More than that, they will change your life.

Most of us think of stewardship as duty. The word itself conjures an image of obligation—paying our tithe, paying our denominational assessments, urging people to give "just a little more" to the church. That kind of thinking locks us into a practice of stewardship that uses outward obedience to mask secret rebellion against God and his way of thinking. So much better is the attitude of John Wesley, who understood the abundance mind-set and practiced open-hearted, openhanded generosity. He taught this regarding personal finances: "Gain all you can. Save all you can. Give all you can."

That is great advice, but generosity does not come naturally to most of us. Our view of stewardship may be better summarized by this twist on Wesley's words: "Earn all you can, can all you get, sit on the lid!" Many good Christians find it difficult to practice true stewardship. In fact, we are trained by the society we live in to think in just the opposite terms about money and financial management. We believe that we'll never have enough. We always need more, and we must cling tightly to the few precious resources we have. Ask a wealthy man "How much money does it take to be happy?" His answer: "Just a little more." That is unfortunate, because generosity is the first law of economics in God's kingdom. When we are generous with what we have, we honor God, impact others, and receive a blessing in the process.

This book is a practical guide for improving not only your personal finances but also your leadership in the area of stewardship. Both you and your congregation will grow stronger financially—and become more effective in ministry—by practicing the principles taught here. We will identify the major obstacles to practicing true stewardship, and you will discover that it is possible to have a complete change of heart in the area of personal and church finances. More than that, you'll learn valuable, practical strategies for making better use of the resources God has given you and your congregation. As you do, you'll discover a new way of thinking about stewardship and a new way of partnering with God in his great plan to reconcile the world to himself.

Here's a preview of what will happen in your life as a result of this new thinking. You will—

- Learn the secrets to successful personal financial management.
- Avoid the single greatest pitfall in personal finances— the prosperity trap.
- Discover the one way to personal financial freedom.
- Gain confidence in your planning for retirement.

Personal finances are a starting point, but they are only part of the picture. To practice true stewardship, your wise management must extend to the church that God has placed under your care. In this book, you will also—

- Create solid financial benchmarks for your church.
- Take the frustration out of church budgeting.
- Ensure that your church makes the most of its resources.
- Learn to generate new funding sources for your ministry.

God doesn't intend for us to be trapped by the standards of this world; he has given us a new way to live, a new way to relate to others—and a new way to think about the resources that he so generously provides. Are you ready for the adventure?

Let's get started!

Part 1

WHOLE LIFE STEWARDSHIP

Seven Things You Must Know to Experience God's Blessing

Stewardship is not merely one aspect of life. As a believer in the God who created heaven and earth, your entire life is about wisely using every resource God has placed within your care—including your body, your time, your talents, and your treasure.

In this section, you will discover the seven things you must know in order to faithfully manage your personal resources and fully experience God's blessing.

1
SIX KEY PRINCIPLES YOU MUST UNDERSTAND ABOUT MONEY

Tim Hansel, in his book *Holy Sweat* tells about an experience he had with his son, Zac. One day the two of them were out in the country, climbing around in some cliffs. Tim Hansel heard his small son yell, "Hey Dad! Catch me!" He turned around to see Zac joyfully jumping off a rock straight at him. The boy had jumped even before he yelled, "Hey Dad!" The dad became a circus act, catching his son in midair, then falling to the ground. After catching his breath, the anxious dad asked in exasperation, "Zac! Can you give me one good reason why you did that?"

The boy responded with remarkable calmness, "Sure . . . because you're my Dad."

Wouldn't it be great to have that kind of confidence in your heavenly Father? Here's the good news. You can! God is trustworthy, and we can have full confidence in him. The secret to practicing authentic stewardship begins with the marvelous discovery that God is trustworthy. He is the source of all that exists. He not only generously provides for his children but also leads us into the adventure of a giving lifestyle.

Scholars point out that Jesus discussed money more than heaven and hell combined, and he talked more about money than did anyone else in the Bible. Financial teacher Howard Dayton has counted 2,350 verses in God's word that deal with money. Pastor Rick Warren suggests that stewardship and redemption are the two themes that encompass the whole of Scripture, from Genesis to Revelation. Clearly, God wants us to have a good understanding of money—what it is, where it comes from, and what we are to do with it. Let's discover six key principles about God and the things he has created.

1. GOD IS THE SOURCE

The very first words of the Bible declare the foundational truth for understanding our world and for practicing stewardship. Although this should be familiar to every one of us, it is a truth often forgotten. "In the beginning God created the heavens and the earth" (Gen. 1:1). That simple statement establishes the first key principle in the life of faith—and stewardship: God is the source of everything.

Time and again God reinforces this truth in Scripture. He declared to the Israelites, "The whole earth is mine" (Ex. 19:5), and he reminds us through the psalmist that "every animal of the forest is mine, and the cattle on a thousand hills" (Ps. 50:10). It is God, not you, who provides air and sunshine, the basic things we need for life, but also food, shelter, clothing, employment, and the resources you need for your family and your congregation.

> **God wants us to have a good understanding of money—what it is, where it comes from, and what we are to do with it.**

When you understand and embrace the idea that God is the source, two things happen. First, you begin to relax. This simple truth takes the stress out of personal and church finances. It's not all up to us; this is God's business. The second result is that you begin to think differently about money, material possessions, and all the resources God has provided. This is the starting point for a generous lifestyle.

2. LOVE IS THE REASON

The second key principle about money is hiding in plain sight. It is the motivation behind God's generosity, and the motivation behind our giving when we are in tune with him. This simple principle is written in what may be the best-known verse in the entire Bible, John 3:16. "For God so loved the world that he *gave* his one and only Son . . ." *(emphasis added)*.

God is generous by nature. He is a giver. He not only created the world and continues to sustain it, but he also freely blesses his creatures with good gifts. This is what the writer of Hebrews tells us: "Anyone who comes to [God] must believe that he exists and that he rewards those who earnestly seek him" (Heb. 11:6). God loves us, and that love motivates his giving. He gave his only Son to gain our freedom from sin, and he continues to give in providing for our needs. Food? Clothing? Shelter? God's Word says, "Your heavenly Father knows that you need them" (Matt. 6:32) and has promised to provide. God loves, therefore God gives.

God's great commands to us are that we should love him and love others. When we love as God loves, we, too, will be motivated to give. God is the source. Love is the reason.

3. REDEMPTION IS THE RESULT

God's giving has a purpose. Remember John 3:16? Let's finish that verse. God gave his only son so "that whoever believes in him shall not perish but have eternal life." God gives to us in order to accomplish something. He gave his son for our freedom. He gives material things to provide for our needs. His generosity has the result of freeing us from sin, from worry, from anxiety about the future (see Matt. 6:33–34). God's giving is motivated by love. God's giving results in our redemption.

4. RESOURCE IS THE EFFECT

The effect of God's giving is amazing, when you stop to think about it. Because we are his beloved children, he has provided us with everything we need. We have adequate resources. Jesus said, "But seek first his kingdom and his righteousness, and all these things will be given to you as well" (Matt. 6:33). "These things" are the very resources we need to thrive in the world—food, shelter, clothing, and the like.

Think about this amazing truth: God has promised to provide us with all we need. We are fully resourced! Though it may not feel that way when you face a stack of bills, we have God's firm promise that he cares about us and provides for us. Rest in the knowledge that God has promised to provide for you "all these things." God's generous giving results in our steady supply.

5. OBEDIENCE IS THE RESPONSE

What is the proper response upon receiving a gift? Every parent can tell you this because they have tried to instill this thinking into their children. When receiving a gift, the proper response is to say "Thank you." Jesus reinforced that truth in a lesson about ten lepers who were cured of their illness. Only one returned to say thanks, and Jesus found that surprising (see Luke 17:11–19). We should be grateful for the gifts God has given to us.

Abraham, our pioneer in the life of faith, demonstrated the best way to put that thankfulness into action. When he encountered the mysterious Melchizedek, who was an early king of Salem (Jerusalem) as well as a priest of God Most High, Abraham became a model for our practice of stewardship. After Melchizedek gave Abraham a generous blessing on behalf of God, the patriarch was moved to respond with thanks. He gave Melchizedek "a tenth of everything" (Gen. 14:20). This spontaneous gesture—tithing, or giving God one tenth of all we have—has become the obedient response of God's people for generations.

God has given us all that we need. He does this because he loves us. Our response? We give in return. We obediently follow God's direction and example by giving both to him and to others. When you realize all that God has done for you, grateful obedience is the only right response.

6. STEWARDSHIP IS THE PROOF

If you remember the first time you drove a car on your own—that is, without a parent or guardian riding with you—it's possible you have heard this admonition, given by countless parents to eager teenage drivers: "Drive it like you own it." That simple command sums up a great truth about stewardship. God owns everything that exists, just as a parent owns a vehicle. Yet God blesses us with full access to his riches, just as a parent may hand over the keys to the family car. The temptation in both cases is to "drive it like you stole it," meaning to be reckless with the gift we've been given. The better response is to treat the gift as if it were your own possession. That does not mean being possessive or stingy. Rather, it means showing proper respect for the gift.

> **When you realize all that God has done for you, grateful obedience is the only right response.**

Our money, our natural resources, our possessions, even our own bodies are not our own. All of this was bought for us at a price, the precious blood of Jesus (see 1 Cor. 6:20). The proof of our gratitude is humble respect for the many gifts that God has provided. We treat them with honor, manage them wisely, and use them carefully because we know that everything belongs to God. Our gratitude for God's generosity will be proven by our wise use of the many gifts he has given.

God is the source. Love is the reason. Redemption is the result. Resource is the effect. Obedience is the response. Stewardship is the proof. Now that you understand these basic principles about money, you're ready for the next lesson—one that you may find surprising indeed.

2
THE ESSENTIAL DIFFERENCE BETWEEN OWNERSHIP AND STEWARDSHIP

In the early morning hours of September 8, 1860, a ship called the Augusta raced out of control through the tumultuous waters of Lake Michigan. Before the captain could shout out the order, the 129-foot schooner smashed into the side of the crowded passenger steamer, The Lady Elgin, which was on its way back to Milwaukee after a night of dinner and dancing in Chicago.

As The Lady Elgin foundered seven miles off the coast of Illinois and slowly broke apart, guests from the steamboat chopped off doors and pieces of the deck to float on. Luckily, the water temperature of Lake Michigan in September is at its warmest. It was still frigid, but a virtual hot bath compared to the below freezing temperatures of late fall and winter. An estimated five hundred survivors were afloat on pieces of The Lady, or treading water as dawn approached.

At daybreak, students from Northwestern University's life-saving squad gathered on the shore and began to rescue the people out of the water who had floated up into the shallows. One brave student, Edward W. Spencer, swam out deep into the waters a total of seventeen times, saving people each time. After his seventeenth trip into the deepest parts of the water, fatigue and delirium set in, and he was taken back to the university where he lay sick in bed for several months. Edward Spencer's health revived, and after graduating from school he moved out to California where he died at the age of eighty-one. A local newspaper reported a tragic fact of this story in his obituary—not one of the people he rescued ever visited Edward to thank him. Not one out of seventeen ever showed him gratitude over a sixty-year period.

One reason for that apparent ingratitude could be the basic misunderstanding of life that has plagued the human race since the time of Adam and Eve. We believe the world and everything in it—especially ourselves, our own lives—belongs to us. We fail to recognize that everything we have, including every day that we live and breathe, is a gift from a gracious God.

We equate the term *owner* with *master*. So when we think of ourselves as "owners" of our homes, our cars, our money, and even our own bodies, we state our belief that we have mastery over all these things. They are ours, and we may do with them as we please. That's the privilege of ownership.

However, when it comes to biblical stewardship of our personal and church resources, there is a huge difference between *ownership* and *stewardship*. Let's review that difference, along with another key term *trusteeship*.

OWNERSHIP

The psalm writer tells us "the earth is the Lord's, and everything in it. The world and all its people belong to him" (Psalm 24:1–2, NLT). That establishes very clearly that we are *not* the owners of the world, it's resources, or even the things we "own." All of it belongs to God. And that brings us to a second key term.

TRUSTEESHIP

In reality, we are trustees of all that God has given to us. We hold it on his behalf and use it for his purposes. In a similar way, the manager of a restaurant is not the owner. He or she merely operates the restaurant on behalf of the real owner, who may never step foot in the door. The manager has no power to sell the property, borrow money on behalf of the business, and may not even be able to hire and fire employees without authorization. The manager's job is to operate the business wisely and profitably, using the resources at hand not for his or her own purposes but to advance the interests of the owner.

Do you see yourself as an owner of your possessions, or as a trustee, holding them on behalf of God? The apostle Paul reminds us, "Do you not know that your bodies are temples of the Holy Spirit, who is in you, whom you have received from God? You are not your own; you were bought at a price. Therefore honor God with your bodies" (1 Cor. 6:19–20). He also writes, "Not that I was ever in need, for I have learned how to be content with whatever I have" (Phil. 4:11, NLT). When you see yourself as a trustee of God's goods, you will more easily be content with what you have.

STEWARDSHIP

God has given us his possessions to manage, and from that allowance we can take what we need. God has promised to supply our daily necessities. Beyond that, we must answer the question of what we will do with the excess? How will we use the excess resources God has entrusted us with? That is the question of stewardship. Scripture teaches, "Give generously . . . and do so without a grudging heart; then because of this the Lord your God will bless you in all your work and in everything you put your hand to." (Deut. 15:10, NLT).

When you see yourself as a manger of your life and not the true owner, it will change the way you think about money, work, possessions, even retirement. Are you a grateful steward, managing on behalf of a gracious God? Or do you tend to be like the rescued boaters, possessive of and ungrateful for the life you've been given? These four questions may help you decide.

1. What do I have?

First, take an inventory of the things you hold. This may take a moment so you may want to reach for a paper and pen. Make a list of all that you have. Start with your life, your health, your family and friends. Think about where you live, what you have eaten already today and what is in your cupboard.

Walk around your house and take an inventory of your possessions. Visit the garage and survey what's there. What about the things that are not at home—your business, your bank accounts, your retirement account? Do you have a list of "your" belongings?

How long is the list? Is there more there than you may have initially thought? Do you have things that you may have forgotten about or no longer need? What does this list tell you about yourself? Now you're ready for the next question.

2. Who owns it?

Who owns the things in your possession? One answer might be "the bank!" Many of us realize that our homes and cars, even some of the consumer goods that we use don't really belong to us but to lending agencies. We don't even "own" all the things we hold title to. Beyond the question of who paid for these things, let's consider the deeper question. Where did they come from, and why do we have them now?

Moses gave this fascinating instruction to the Israelites. He said, "Remember the LORD your God, for it is he who gives you the ability to produce wealth, and so confirms his covenant, which he swore to your ancestors, as it is today" (Deut. 8:18). We have what we have only because God has given it to us. Even when we "earned" it ourselves, it was really God who enabled us to do that. Everything we have comes from him. God owns it all.

3. How much do I need?

The apostle Paul had many ups and downs in life. He was at one time quite wealthy and comfortable, but his mission for Jesus took him to difficult places—persecution, shipwreck, even imprisonment. Yet near the end of his life he wrote these encouraging words: "For we brought nothing into the world, and we can take nothing out of it. But if we have food and clothing, we will be content with that" (1 Tim. 6:8).

Thinking of Paul's life and words, go back over your inventory of belongings and ask this question: How many of these things do I truly need? That word *need* can play tricks on us. We often confuse it with another word, *want*. Many of the things we think we need are really luxuries or, at best, conveniences.

To understand the difference between ownership and stewardship—between mastery and management—return to the example of the restaurant manager. In a busy kitchen or crowded dining room, unnecessary items are not a luxury but an impediment to good service. Apply that thinking to your life and stewardship. Which of your possessions are enabling you to serve God more fully, and which have become distractions or, worse, deterrents to doing God's will?

And that brings us to the final question.

4. How will I respond?

New insight requires new actions or behaviors. What will you do with your newfound knowledge about God, yourself, and the management of his belongings? Will you continue to act like an owner, using and disposing of your money, your possessions, your time, and even your health as if you were accountable to no one? Or, recognizing that God, not you, is the true owner of your life, will you manage your time, talent, and treasure to meet his purposes? Your answer to that question will largely determine the quality of your stewardship.

Now that you understand the essential difference between ownership and stewardship, you're ready for the next lesson in managing on God's behalf. It concerns one of the most basic errors we can make in thinking of stewardship. This rookie mistake is easy to make because it centers on the one thing we're sure God must want for everyone: prosperity.

3

THE PROSPERITY TRAP

A man once came to Peter Marshall, former chaplain of the United States Senate, with a concern about tithing. "I have a problem," he said. "I have been tithing for some time. It wasn't too bad when I was making $20,000 a year; I could afford to give up $2,000. But now that I am making $500,000, there is no way I can afford to give away $50,000 a year."

Peter Marshall reflected on this wealthy man's dilemma but gave no advice. He simply said, "Yes, sir. I see that you have a problem. I think we ought to pray about it. Is that all right?"

The man agreed, so Dr. Marshall bowed his head and prayed, "Dear Lord, this man has a problem, and I pray that you will help him. Please reduce his salary back to the place where he can afford to tithe."[1]

We may laugh at the wealthy man whom Dr. Marshall so kindly put in his place; but the man's attitude reveals something that many of us are tempted to believe about God, money, and ourselves. Without realizing it, we may fall

---
1. Kevin G. Harney, *Seismic Shifts* (Zondervan, 2005)

into the prosperity trap: the belief that God wants nothing more desperately than for us to be wealthy, and that poverty is some sort of sin.

Let's take a closer look at this flawed thinking so that you can learn to spot the prosperity trap and discover the better blessing that God has for you—his presence.

WHAT PROSPERITY IS AND ISN'T

First, let's talk about what prosperity is—and what it isn't. Many people have the idea that prosperity means having more than what we need. If we have an excess of everything—money, time, possessions, food—then we are "rich," therefore prosperous. Jesus once told a story to illustrate the flaw in that thinking (see Luke 12:13–21). Jesus introduced the story with an urgent warning: "Watch out! Be on your guard against all kinds of greed; life does not consist in an abundance of possessions" (v. 15). He went on to tell of a certain rich farmer whose crops were so abundant that he began scheming of ways to store even more grain and make even more money. The man figured that since he was now prosperous, he could take life easy. "But God said to him, 'You fool! This very night your life will be demanded from you. Then who will get what you have prepared for yourself?'" (v. 20). Jesus concluded the story with another dire warning: "This is how it will be with whoever stores up things for themselves but is not rich toward God" (vv. 16–17).

Prosperity is not having an abundance of money, goods, or time. It is enjoying God's presence and blessing in a right relationship with him. Prosperous people are those who have all they need, not necessarily all they could ever have imagined. And the chief blessing of a prosperous life is God himself. It is having a right relationship with him through Jesus Christ. If you have that, you have everything. If you don't have that, nothing else matters. And if you have food and a place to stay, you have more than enough (see 1 Tim. 6:8). The prosperity trap is mistaking your own wealth and security above a right relationship with God. Avoid it at all costs!

> **_Prosperity is not having an abundance of money, goods, or time. It is enjoying God's presence and blessing in a right relationship with him._**

THE CAUSE OF POVERTY

We fall into the mistake of placing too much value on our own wealth and security in part because we misunderstand what prosperity really is—and also because we have a false idea of what it means to be poor. Most of us think of being poor as having little or no money and possessions. Certainly, those who lack adequate food and shelter are poor in that sense. Literal poverty abounds. Consider these global statistics:

- 2.8 billion people live on less than two dollars per day.
- 1.3 billion live on less than one dollar per day.
- 1.3 billion have no access to clean water.
- 2.25 billion have no sanitation facilities.
- 790 million go to bed hungry every night.
- 1.5 billion have no access to health care.
- 1.6 billion have never heard the gospel.

Contrast those facts with the amazing wealth held by North America. Though comprising only 4 percent of the world's population, we hold 40 percent of the world's wealth. Fully 80 percent of the wealth held by evangelical Christians is within North America. That is most likely more than enough to fund the fulfillment of the Great Commission.

That stark contrast points to another kind of poverty, one that can be experienced by even the wealthiest people. This is poverty of spirit. Remember Jesus' words in the parable of the rich fool. It is possible to be incredibly wealthy in terms of money or possessions but not to be "rich toward God" (Luke

12:21). Jesus warned also about the danger of storing up treasure on earth, that is, material wealth, versus treasure in heaven, meaning our relationships with God (see Matt. 6:19–21). Material wealth often leads to poverty of spirit. Of the two types of poverty, the latter is far more dangerous.

Imagine two people with very different financial circumstances. One has a spacious suburban home, two late-model cars, a cupboard filled with food, and a growing retirement account. Yet this person worries constantly about money, never feels that he has enough, and anxiously compares himself to his neighbor, who appears to "have it made." His heart is filled with envy, greed, and resentment. Is this person rich?

Now think of a person who lives in humble circumstances. Her meager income barely pays for food and rent. All of her clothing comes from a second-hand shop, and she owns no car. Yet she has friends who share with her, has food and shelter every day, and enjoys her work. Her heart is filled with gratitude toward God and others. Is this person poor?

It is certainly true that starvation and homelessness are true miseries, often caused by human injustice. Yet the poverty many of us deal with is a poverty of spirit caused by the mistaken belief that we never have enough. In fact, God has promised to provide our daily necessities as we place our trust in him and put his will ahead of ours. "Seek first his kingdom and his righteousness, and all these things will be given to you as well" (Matt. 6:33). This is true prosperity.

ARE YOU RICH OR POOR?

So what about you, are you rich or poor? Do you have enough to eat each day? Have you a place to sleep at night? Has God provided for your daily needs and perhaps a bit more? Are you content with that? The answer to that last question is also the answer to the first. As the apostle Paul put it, "Godliness with contentment is great gain" (1 Tim. 6:6). This is true prosperity.

Having a right attitude toward finances is the first step to total stewardship. But stewardship involves more than finances and possessions. We will learn about that in the next chapter—if you can spare the time.

4
THE HIDDEN VALUE OF TIME

For most of his lifetime, the achievements of former U.S. President Bill Clinton were remarkable for one thing: his young age. Clinton was just thirty years old when he became attorney general of Arkansas. Only two years later, he was elected governor of Arkansas, the youngest person in history to hold such a position. At the youthful age of forty-four, he was elected President, the second-youngest person to hold the oval office.

Yet in August 2006, during his sixtieth birthday celebration, the reflective former president admitted that his life had changed. Though he had once been a youthful politician, playing the saxophone for eager MTV audiences, the white-haired Clinton is reported to have said, "For most of my working life, I was the youngest person doing what I was doing. Then one day I woke up and I was the oldest person in every room. In just a few days, I will be sixty years old. I hate it, but it's true."[2] The former chief executive took sixty years to learn the most obvious yet remarkable thing about time: it goes by quickly.

Most of us don't think about the fact that each day we are given ten gross

---

2. "I'm 60 and I Hate It: Bill Clinton," *Breitbart.com* (August 15, 2006), http://www.breitbart.com/news/2006/08/15/060815185415.fesfqduy.html.

of the most remarkable things God has created. Every morning we wake up with 1,440 minutes deposited in our account. Like dollars, we can spend them any way we choose. We can waste them, hoard them, invest them, or let them pass idly through our hands. Time, like money, is a precious commodity that God has given us to manage. And here's the most amazing thing: We have all the time there is. Others may have more money, better health, or greater material resources, but every person has exactly the same amount of time to spend every single day.

> **You cannot hope to manage God's resources wisely without knowing the mind and heart of the One who created them.**

Make no mistake, time is a commodity that God expects us to manage well. Do you remember Jesus' parable of the talents (see Matt. 25:14–30)? The story involves a master who entrusted his three servants with sums of money to invest during his absence. Two of the servants invested wisely and earned interest. The master commended them upon his return. The third servant, the one who had the least to invest, did nothing with it. The master condemned this lazy servant for his inaction. The point of the story is not that we should lend money at interest but that we should be faithful with opportunities, making the most of our time. Jesus will return one day, and he expects to find us diligently using our time for his purposes. We are to be good stewards of our time.

How well are you managing the time God has given you? Let's review the key areas where you must invest time wisely to produce remarkable results in your life and ministry.

GOD

Your relationship with God is the most important one in your life, and as with every relationship it can only be cultivated through time. What does your use of time reveal about the state of your spiritual health? When, where, and for how long do you spend time listening to God? Do you feel a sense of closeness with God on a daily basis? How much time do you devote to pursuing God daily through personal spiritual disciplines? You cannot hope to manage God's resources wisely without knowing the mind and heart of the One who created them.

SELF

The next key area to invest time is you. Though it may sound counterintuitive, this time must come second in your life, even ahead of others. If you are not in good health physically, mentally, emotionally, and, above all, spiritually, you will be unable to manage God's resources well in other areas of your life. Self-care is part of a balanced life, and this is essential for anyone in Christian ministry. Here are some questions to diagnose your stewardship of personal time.

- Are you frequently tired? How much sleep do you get on average?
- What is your daily form of exercise? Yes, daily.
- Do your eating habits reflect a balanced, healthy approach to food?
- When was the last time you learned something based on personal interest or self-enrichment rather than for work?
- Do you have a hobby? What do you do for leisure?
- What fuels you? How often do you do that?

Investing time in yourself will pay huge dividends in your family, your professional life, and your ministry. If you are unhealthy, stressed, tired, and running on empty, you cannot make the most of the opportunities—both financially and professionally—that God brings your way.

Is your use of personal time within balance? If not, what needs to change?

FAMILY AND FRIENDS

If you are blessed to have a spouse, children, or extended family, these are the most important relationships in your life. Your closest friends are included in this area of time management also. Giving time to these relationships is not a luxury: It is essential for your health and the health of your ministry. Your family is the first arena in which God calls you to be a faithful manager of his resources. That includes both material goods and the most precious resources you have been given—yourself. Here are a few questions to diagnose your stewardship of family time:

- How much time per day do you spend in meaningful interaction with family and friends?
- Would your children say that you are "always working"?
- How often do you spend extended periods of time with family and friends, such as an all-day experience or a vacation?
- Do you find yourself annoyed by interruptions from your spouse, children, or extended family?
- Do you have family rituals that involve spending time together, such as a date night or movie night?
- Can you name three close friends outside your ministry context? How often do you spend time with them?

Family and friends are neither a luxury nor a distraction from your real life. They represent the most crucial first step in your stewardship of time outside your personal life—that is, your investment in others. Does your use of family and friends time reveal a healthy balance? If not, name one thing you can do to bring change in that area.

WORK

Everyone who must earn a living—which is just about everyone—must give diligent attention to work. This is not merely a matter of seeking wealth or success; God expects us to invest our time wisely in order to provide for others and ourselves. The writer of Proverbs offers this blunt warning: "A little sleep, a little slumber, a little folding of the hands to rest—and poverty will come on you like a thief and scarcity like an armed man" (Prov. 6:10–11). Many people work well over forty hours per week, which may be necessary to give adequate attention to your work. Consistently working sixty or more hours may be a cause for concern. In fact, it may be counterproductive because we become less effective when tired or stressed.

Is your use of time for work in balance, neither too much nor too little? If not, what can you do to correct that?

> **When you give your first and best time to the most critical areas, you will have more time and energy to invest elsewhere.**

MINISTRY

Ministry time is work time for those who are employed by the church. However, even pastors and others in ministry can serve in ways other than their professional capacity. Each one of us is gifted and called to serve. If we do not invest some of our time in ministry, we are not fully honoring God's gift of time, just as if we do not give a portion of our income to the Lord, we are not being faithful with his gift of money. What is your ministry? How much time do you devote to serving others in this way? Is that time in balance? If not, how can you restore balance?

EVERYTHING ELSE

After God, self, family and friends, work, and ministry comes everything else. There will always be demands on your time outside these key areas, but they'll pay lower dividends on your attention. Give proper priority to the first things, and the other uses of your time are sure to be in balance.

Proper stewardship of time is based on a solid set of priorities. When you give your first and best time to the most critical areas, you will have more time and energy to invest elsewhere. You cannot create time or multiply it, but you can make yourself more effective in the things you do by managing time well. And that's exactly what God wants you to do.

And there's one more resource you must manage well in order to maximize your time. What is it? You probably already know because the answer is inside of you.

5
HOW TO MAXIMIZE YOUR TALENTS

Jenny Thompson has earned more medals than any American woman in Olympic competition. Over the course of three Olympic games, she earned ten medals in swimming. That is more medals than have been earned by any other Olympic swimmer of any nation. Eight of the medals were gold medals.

However, Jenny didn't win a gold medal in any individual event. All the golds were in team events. That has caused some to question whether this highly decorated athlete belongs in the pantheon of true Olympic greats. After all, three other swimmers contributed to each of those gold medals.

The young swimmer from Dove, New Hampshire, seems to have pondered the question herself. She said, "It's got to be very different to experience an individual gold versus a team gold." And ice-skating champion Bonnie Blair said recently of Jenny," I wish she could feel what it's like for an individual gold, to witness it by herself and not just as part of a team."[3]

---
3. "Jenny Thompson's Gold-Medal Teamwork," *citing John Mutchler, AP reports (September 2000), PreachingToday.com, accessed April 15, 2015,* http://www.preachingtoday.com/illustrations/2000/october/12649.html.

Those sentiments reveal a common misunderstanding about one of the greatest resources God has given to each of us—our talents. We tend to value only the most visible achievements of highly talented solo performers. In fact, God has gifted each of us with three types of abilities, and each person has a significant contribution to make to God's kingdom, whether as a solo performer, part of a winning team, or a backstage volunteer.

God has given you:

- Natural Talents
- Acquired Abilities
- Spiritual Gifts

Total stewardship involves using each of them wisely and well for God's glory. Your first step will be to take an inventory of the resources with which God has blessed you.

NATURAL TALENTS

Everyone is born with some natural capacities. While it is true that some people appear to be more agile than others, and a few seem to have been standing behind the door when the Lord handed out common sense, nearly everyone has natural talents in at least four areas.

Mental Talents. You don't have to be a genius to have mental talents that can be used for your good and God's glory. What is your level of natural gifting in terms of mental capacity?

Physical Talents. Though they will diminish with age, your strength, agility, dexterity, and stamina are tremendous assets.

Social Talents. Charm, politeness, extroversion, and even the "gift of gab," are natural capacities or abilities that you may have to a greater degree than others do. What will you do with them?

Creative Talents. Some people are blessed with the vision, capacity, or skill to create—music, art, ideas. Leadership, too, is a creative natural talent.

ACQUIRED ABILITIES

Beyond the things you are "born with," you have abilities that you've acquired over years of living. Take an inventory of your acquired skills. They fall into at least three categories.

Formal Education. If you are fortunate enough to have completed a high school, college, or graduate degree, you are among the world's elite in terms of education. What knowledge, skills, or insights have you acquired through education?

Experience. Formal education isn't the only context in which learning happens. The "school of hard knocks" has matriculated a good many students also. Work, marriage, raising children, travel, and even hardships, such as grief or illness, have enriched you with knowledge and skill. What have you learned from your experiences?

Observation. Self-teaching is another way in which you have likely developed or added to your natural abilities. The apostle Paul urged his young protégé, Timothy, "The things you have heard me say in the presence of many witnesses entrust to reliable people who will also be qualified to teach others" (2 Tim. 2:2). In other words, *Listen, keep your eyes open, and pass along what you know!* What are the best practices you have learned for your work, your family, and your life?

SPIRITUAL GIFTS

The most important, and possibly the most mysterious, abilities God has given us as a resource are spiritual gifts. Yet many Christians do not understand or use their spiritual gifts. These action steps will help you become a better steward of the spiritual gifts God has for you.

Believe the Promise. Spiritual gifts are clearly promised in Scripture. The apostle Paul listed various gifts and taught the early churches about them in Romans 12, 1 Corinthians 12, and Ephesians 4. Educate yourself concerning the gifts, and trust that the Spirit also has a gift or gifts for you.

See What You Have. God asked Moses a seemingly obvious question in Exodus 4:2: "What is that in your hand?" The question was meant to point out to Moses that the very thing he already had—a staff—would be an instrument of God's power. What do you have? What gifting seems apparent to you? What do others see in you?

Seek the Spirit. Do not be idle concerning the discovery and use of your gifts.

Seek the Spirit.

Ask for God's help.

Study the Scripture.

Listen for God's voice.

Accept Authority. As a child, Jesus learned obedience while working in the carpenter's shop (see Luke 2:49). Accept the direction of your pastor or spiritual authorities. What have they asked you to do? How might your gifting become apparent through this?

Seek Opportunities. Spiritual gifts are not museum pieces or mere theoretical concepts. They emerge when put into practice. Seek opportunities to serve in ways that challenge you spiritually yet excite your imagination. Watch for your spiritual gifts to take shape.

Total stewardship includes your personal finances, of course, and your time. It includes your abilities as well. God has given you all that you are. Are you using your body, mind, and spirit in ways that honor him fully?

Total stewardship involves wise use of your time and talent as well as your money. But what is stewardship for? Why does God ask us to use our resources carefully? The answer is simple: We've got work to do. Stewardship is about creating impact through the resources God has given you. In the next chapter, we will discover three simple steps for doing just that.

6
THREE STEPS TO CREATING FINANCIAL IMPACT

Brennan Manning, in his book, *The Ragamuffin Gospel*, tells the story of Fiorello LaGuardia, the mayor of New York City during the Great Depression and World War II. Fiorello was a well-loved and respected mayor of the Big Apple. He was known for his cheerful disposition and enthusiasm. The story goes that one cold night in January, Mr. LaGuardia visited a night court in the poorest section of the city and relieved the judge from his bench to preside over the night's cases. One of the first cases was against an old lady who had stolen a loaf of bread. She pleaded with LaGuardia that her husband had left her, and her daughter and grandchildren were starving. The mayor took pity on her situation, but the shopkeeper was insistent and would not drop the charges, wanting to prove a point to other hungry thieves. LaGuardia knew he had to punish her to be just, so he fined her ten dollars.

Before the woman could explain that she didn't have any money, mayor LaGuardia took a ten-dollar bill from his wallet and paid the fine. But he didn't stop there. He proceeded to fine everyone in the courtroom fifty cents for living in a town where a single mother had to steal bread to feed her starving children and grandchildren. The woman left the courtroom with $47.50.

Perhaps we should all be fined for living in a world where children go to bed hungry and our neighbors' needs go unmet. There is a major theme running through the Bible that calls for us to care for the poor, the widow, and the orphan. In Leviticus 19:10, the Lord commanded the Israelites to not go over their fields twice so that the fallen grain would be left for the poor and the hungry. Numerous times in the book of Deuteronomy, God commanded the children of Israel to fight for the cause of the fatherless and the widow.

In other words, we are given resources not for our good alone but also for the good of others. We are to create *impact* through our stewardship. Total stewardship is not merely about using money wisely so that you have enough. It is about using what God has given us to accomplish his purposes.

As we have mentioned, John Wesley coined a marvelous three-step plan for creating that impact in his sermon called "The Use of Money." Though often misquoted, the actual words of Wesley's dictum are these: "Gain all you can. Save all you can. Give all you can."[4] Follow these simple steps, and you will change the world. Let's take a closer look.

1. GAIN ALL YOU CAN

There's a common misconception among Christians that money, in and of itself, is evil. In fact it is not. Like so many other things in life, money is neutral, neither good nor bad. What the Bible does say is that "the love of money is a root of all kinds of evil" (1 Tim. 6:10). We need not look far to see examples of both wealthy and poor people who have been destroyed by their desire for the world's wealth. Simply having money, however, is not a sin. On the contrary, the Bible urges us to be diligent and industrious so that we can provide for others and ourselves. The Proverbs urge us to "Go to the ant, you sluggard; consider its ways and be wise!" (Prov. 6:6). The implication is that we should be like these tiniest of creatures, busily at work gathering resources.

---

4. John Wesley, "The Use of Money," *The Works of the Reverend John Wesley*, 3rd ed., vol. vi (Kansas City, Mo.: Beacon Hill Press of Kansas City, 1979), 124.

How diligent are you at gathering resources? Do you seek ways to earn? Do you find ways to reuse and recycle items that you no longer need? Do you take opportunities to gain extra income? To use resources, you must first possess them. Gain all you can.

2. SAVE ALL YOU CAN

Next, save all you can. This is the point at which many of us fail, and therefore fail to have an impact on the world. We spend too much of what we gain, usually on ourselves. Worse, we often borrow beyond our means so that we can spend even more. Recent statistics reveal that the average North American household has $15,611 in credit card debt, a mortgage of $155,192, and $32,264 in student loan debt. It is no wonder that most Christians don't tithe—they're already spending more money than they earn.

Are you currently in debt? Do you have a growing balance on your credit card accounts? Do you feel encumbered by the many payments and obligations you have taken on? To practice total stewardship, you must turn those numbers around and move from acquiring debt to acquiring wealth. The only way to do that is to spend less than you earn. Save all you can.

We are given resources not for our good alone but also for the good of others.

3. GIVE ALL YOU CAN

Here is the point where impact happens—the place where needs and resources meet. When you have acquired excess resources by diligent work and careful saving, you are in a position to make an impact on the world. Remember that the point of total stewardship is not simply for you to live comfortably. It is for you to manage God's wealth on his behalf. Give all you can.

It has been estimated that enough resources are already in the hands of Christians to complete the Great Commission—taking the gospel to every nation—within our lifetime. But that can't happen until we are willing to seize the opportunity and give. Vision is not enough to reach a goal, however great. Resources are also required.

What could you accomplish if you were able to give a full tithe: 10 percent of your income? What could you accomplish if you could double that amount by careful saving and spending? What if you were able to increase your income and save half of it, freeing a full 50 percent of your earning power to feed the hungry, house the homeless, and carry the gospel to those who need forgiveness and peace? The secret to making an impact is really no secret at all. Gain all you can. Save all you can. Give all you can.

Have you ever wondered why some people always seem to have more than enough and can give generously while others constantly feel that they never have quite enough? That is because there is one thing generous people know that others don't. We will reveal that secret in the next chapter.

7
THE ONE THING GENEROUS PEOPLE KNOW

If you ever find yourself crossing Nevada's Armargosa Desert, you may come across an old hand pump along one of the very long and seldom-used trails. It is said that this pump offers the only hope of gaining drinking water for miles around, and that if you look closely you'll find a letter tucked inside a baking-powder can and wired to the handle of the pump. The letter reads as follows:

This pump is all right as of June 1932. I put a new sucker washer into it and it ought to last five years. But the washer dries out and the pump has got to be primed. Under the white rock I buried a bottle of water, out of the sun and cork end up. There's enough water in it to prime the pump, but not if you drink some first. Pour about one-fourth and let her soak to wet the leather. Then pour in the rest medium fast and pump like crazy. You'll git water. The well has never run dry. Have faith. When you git watered up, fill the bottle and put it back like you found it for the next feller. (signed) Desert Pete. P.S. Don't go drinking the water first. Prime the pump with it and you'll git all you can hold.

The legend of Desert Pete reveals a valuable lesson, and one that every generous person has already learned. In order to gain more of God's resources, you must give some away. In other words, God rewards generosity. Resources flow to those who use them well.

This principle is revealed in Scripture and reinforced by Jesus himself. God said, through the prophet Malachi, "'Bring the whole tithe into the storehouse, that there may be food in my house. Test me in this,' says the Lord Almighty, 'and see if I will not throw open the floodgates of heaven and pour out so much blessing that there will not be room enough to store it'" (Mal. 3:10). Nowhere else in Scripture does God invite us to call his bluff, to "test" him! He promises to bless those who practice good stewardship, which includes generous giving.

Resources flow to those who use them well.

Jesus made a similar point when he said, "Give, and it will be given to you. A good measure, pressed down, shaken together and running over, will be poured into your lap" (Luke 6:38). That is the result you can expect, and Jesus also gave the principle behind it: "For with the measure you use, it will be measured to you." When you trust God by giving away what you have for his purposes, he provides even more.

There are countless examples of this both in Scripture and in more recent times. Remember Elijah and the widow who lived in Zarephath (see 1 Kings 17:7–16)? The woman had just a small amount of oil and flour and was about to prepare a last meal for herself and her starving son. Elijah asked her to demonstrate faith by preparing a meal for him first, which she did. As a result, the small amount of food that she had left miraculously did not run out while the country endured a great famine. When we give to God first, he multiplies our resources.

That's what a modern-day mom named Tanya also discovered. Listen to her story:

> *Stewardship is more than giving money. For me it is a way of life. When I give my time or talent, as well as my tithe through the local church I experience Christian community. It begins with my weekly offering. Paying my tithe, I obey the Word of God and as a result, I find myself growing in my relationship with Jesus Christ. When I give my time and talent in volunteering, I find my life is being enriched through those I minister to, and through those I minister with. I am growing in my own faith as I help others grow in theirs.*
>
> *For many years, I was a receiver and not a giver. I attended the services of my church and put a few dollars in the offering, but I never really felt like I was a "part" of the church. One Sunday my pastor challenged the congregation to give their whole life to God. He said being a manager of the things God blessed us with is being a steward of our money, our abilities, and our time. I accepted the challenge. Let's just say, I finally got it! God began to bless my finances when I began to set aside a tenth of my income as an offering to him. I began to feel more confident about myself and my abilities when I began to use my time and talents in ministry. And the bonus? I finally felt like I was a vital part of my church.*

I can't imagine not being busy in helping out in church. I can't imagine missing out on the blessing of serving God with my giving. I can't imagine keeping all my time to myself, and not using it as a way of helping those in need. God's Word is true. It really is more blessed to give than to receive.

Why do some people give generously even though they seem to have little while many "rich" people feel poor? Generous givers have discovered this amazing secret: God blesses generosity. Resources flow to those who use them well. This is the way total stewardship works.

Now that you have an understanding of the principles of total stewardship, you are ready to put those ideas into action. It is time to manage your money.

Part 2

PERSONAL FINANCES

Your Ten Step Roadmap to Financial Freedom

Just as faith without works is useless, so the principles of total stewardship will be meaningless to you without a solid plan for action. The remainder of this book is devoted to helping you apply those principles in your personal life and in your ministry.

The first step is to create a roadmap to your personal financial freedom.

8
DEVELOPING A FINANCIAL ROADMAP

When you look at the state of your personal finances, you may feel overwhelmed and discouraged. See if any of this sounds familiar:

- You have more debt than you ever wanted, and the payments are getting harder to make.
- It feels as if you never have enough to go around.
- You know you cannot afford a vacation, but you need a break so badly that you charge your trip on a credit card.
- You do not talk about finances much with your spouse because the conversations are always stressful.
- If that sounds like your financial reality, take heart. Many others have experienced this, and there is hope.

During my (Larry Moore's) junior and senior years at Bible college, my wife, Karin, and I worked as foster parents, taking care of abused and delinquent boys. I also served as youth pastor at one of the churches nearby.

In the summertime I operated my own house painting business to earn some extra cash. When we graduated from college, our household income was approximately $38,000 per year. That was pretty good for a couple of college students in the early 1980s.

After graduation I accepted my first full-time ministry assignment, and the starting salary was $6,900—per year. Though some pastoral positions include housing or a housing allowance, this one did not. We were responsible for our own housing and utilities on that salary. Talk about a crash course in personal financial management! We learned a great deal about managing personal finances during those early years of ministry. These chapters in part two distill that learning into ten steps that anyone can follow, regardless of income level. This is your roadmap to financial freedom.

STEP 1. PUT FIRST THINGS FIRST

The first step to financial freedom may seem counterintuitive, but it is both biblically and practically sound. You start by giving your money away. Acknowledge that God has first priority in your life by offering him the first fruits of your labor. Tithing on your income, or giving one-tenth to the Lord, is the first step to financial peace.

Jesus said, "But seek first his kingdom and his righteousness, and all these things will be given to you as well" (Matt. 6:33). God has promised to take care of us when we devote our first and best energy to him. Nothing does that better than tithing. Malachi reminds, urges us to "'bring the whole tithe into the storehouse, that there may be food in my [God's] house. Test me in this,' says the Lord Almighty, 'and see if I will not throw open the floodgates of heaven and pour out so much blessing that you will not have room enough for it'" (Mal. 3:10). When we demonstrate our faith by putting God first in our finances, we place ourselves on the road to financial freedom. Put God first in your personal finances by tithing on your income to God through your local church on a regular basis.

STEP 2. PLAN FOR THE UNEXPECTED

It has been said that when you fail to plan, you plan to fail. That is especially true in the area of personal finances. When you do not plan for emergencies, it is as if you are planning to have an emergency. When you do plan, you take much of the stress out of the unexpected events that invariably crop up. Begin by creating an emergency fund. Put away at least $500 to $1,000 for short-term emergencies such as car repairs, emergency travel, and the like. Replenish the fund as needed from unexpected income such as tax refunds, salary bonuses, or part-time work. Having this money available will even out your cash flow—and calm your nerves—when unexpected expenses arise.

> **When we demonstrate our faith by putting God first in our finances, we place ourselves on the road to financial freedom.**

STEP 3. DEVELOP A SPENDING PLAN

The word *budget* sounds ominous, and many people have an aversion to creating a personal budget. They think it will be like wearing a financial straightjacket, taking the joy out of earning and spending money. In fact the opposite is true. A budget is nothing more than a spending plan. It puts you in control of your money. Without a budget, impulse spending or spending on things other than your highest priorities will take you out of financial balance. Here are five simple steps to making a personal budget:

1. Begin with your values. Determine what is important to you and be sure those things are reflected in your plan.

2. Determine your net income. This is your "take home pay," not including bonuses, overtime, and the like.

3. Identify fixed expenses. Fixed expenses are the recurring bills you must pay every month, quarter or year: things like a mortgage and utilities.

4. List discretionary expenses. Discretionary spending is the money you can choose to save or spend on whatever you wish after your fixed expenses are met.

5. Create a spending plan that has positive cash flow. In other words, tinker with the discretionary amounts (or reduce fixed expenses) so that your income is greater than your expenses.

Now that you have a spending plan, you'll need to manage it by paying consistent attention to your spending, making adjustments as needed. Here are the three things you should do every month to manage your spending plan and stay on budget:

1. *Balance your accounts regularly.* You can do this with a checkbook and pen, or use financial software that is readily available, or even your online banking site. Review your statement to see that you are spending within the plan.

2. *Manage monthly cash flow.* The budget will list total income and expenses for the month. However, the due dates for your bills may not align exactly with your paydays. Plan your spending so that you will have adequate cash on hand when each bill is due.

3. *Review your budget at the end of each month.* If you've gotten off track, make a plan for avoiding that in the future.

Also, think through the month ahead and forecast any unusual income or expenses that may be on the horizon.

Finally, consider getting one month ahead with your expenses to make cash flow management easier. That may seem like an impossible goal, but with wise saving and careful planning, you can get there.

STEP 4. ELIMINATE DEBT

Debt is the *spare tire* most people drag around wherever they go. It prevents generous giving, limits financial choices, and causes needless anxiety. Get rid of debt as quickly as you can. Make a concentrated effort to retire one debt at a time, beginning with the smallest one and moving to the largest. Make minimum payments on other debts while you pay each one off one by one, again, beginning with the smallest.

Consider consolidating debts with a home equity loan, if you have adequate equity in your home and interest rates are favorable. Be careful of getting "upside down" on your home, however, by borrowing more money than you could sell it for, including all selling costs. Do not take on more debt during this time. After you have retired smaller debts such as credit card balances, you will be ready to take on larger items such as your auto loan or even your mortgage. Just keep paying off debts until they are gone.

STEP 5. CREATE A LONG-TERM EMERGENCY FUND

Your emergency fund of $500 to $1,000 will get you through a small problem such as a car repair. But for larger emergencies such as a job loss or disability, you will need more financial strength. When you are debt free (not including your mortgage debt), begin funding your long-term emergency fund. You will want to set aside one- to-three months' worth of your net income. Use funds previously allocated for short-term debt until this fund is fully funded, then direct those funds back to retiring major debts such as your mortgage.

STEP 6. PUT MONEY INTO PERSONAL SAVINGS

According to the U.S. Commerce Department, the rate of personal savings in 2006 was a negative 1 percent. That means that people actually had less money in savings at the end of the year than at the beginning. It was the worst since 1933, the height of the Great Depression. To have financial freedom, you need personal savings. Make savings a line item in your spending plan, treating it as a fixed expense. Set a specific goal for personal savings. Many people choose 10 percent, just like tithing. Your personal savings can be directed in a number of ways, including your long-term emergency fund, vacation expenses, education, major purchases, discretionary giving, or investing. To earn a higher than average rate of interest with a savings organization that invests in projects you would be proud to support, check out Wesleyan Investment Foundation at wifonline.com.

STEP 7. MINIMIZE RISK WITH INSURANCE

Some risks are too great for the average person to prepare for on his or her own. Insurance is a tool for managing those major risks by sharing them with others. Here are some types of insurance you should consider:

Disability Insurance is used to replace income for a family in the event that one of the wage earners is disabled.

Life Insurance offsets the loss of income experienced when a family wage earner dies prematurely or unexpectedly. It is also used to balance estates and provide liquidity for estate planning purposes.

Health Insurance protects family income and assets in the event of a catastrophic health care need due to injury or illness.

Property Insurance protects important personal assets such as a home, an auto, and household furnishings, which would be difficult to replace in the event of loss.

Liability Insurance protects from loss of assets in the event of an adverse legal judgment.

Long Term Care Insurance preserves family income and assets when extended health care is needed.

In addition to considering these forms of insurance, you might consider reducing insurance premiums by accepting a higher deductible. Self-fund the deductible through your emergency fund.

There really is no mystery to personal financial freedom. It is a matter of having a sound plan and working that plan consistently. Make a roadmap to your financial future; follow it every month, and you will get there.

Managing your day-to-day expenses is a big part of total stewardship, but it is not the only element of a sound personal financial strategy. To be a total steward, you've got to begin thinking about the future, including your retirement. In the next chapter, we will learn how to do exactly that.

9

THE HOW AND WHY OF RETIREMENT PLANNING

STEP 8. SAVING FOR RETIREMENT

Retirement is close at hand for the 77 million people born between 1946 and 1965, otherwise known as baby boomers. However, the anti-aging industry is booming as the last century's teen generation grows more desperate to stay young. . . . The American Academy of Anti-Aging Medicine reports that the anti-aging industry annually garners tens of billions of dollars per year, and more than 1,500 doctors have been certified as anti-aging practitioners.[5]

Yet no amount of medical treatment, nor any investment of dollars, however large, can stop the inevitable march of time. We may not like to admit that we are growing older, but we are all on a one-way street toward retirement. Like it or not, each of us must face the reality that we will not stay young forever. At some point, we will need to slow down or stop working entirely. The wise person prepares for that eventuality through careful retirement planning.

---

5. Arlene Weintraub, "Selling the Promise of Youth," *Bloomberg Business*, March 19, 2006, accessed April 20, 2015, http://www.bloomberg.com/bw/stories/2006-03-19/selling-the-promise-of-youth.

No matter where you are in your life cycle, you can save and invest for the future.

Whether you are a young person just beginning your career, or a middle-ager beginning your fourth quarter, you can effectively plan for your retirement period. Here are some simple ways to take the mystery out of future financial planning.

BEGIN NOW

The very best time to begin planning for your retirement is yesterday. Many people realize that, which makes the prospect of starting now seem pointless. After all, if I'm already behind the curve, why start now? However, the second-best day to begin planning for retirement is today! No matter where you are in your life cycle, you can save and invest for the future.

One reason to begin as soon as you can is the miracle of compound interest. It's really no miracle, of course, just simple arithmetic. But the effect of compound interest seems miraculous over time. When you leave your money on deposit with a financial institution, you will earn a rate of interest. Let's use 8 percent as an example. So if you were to invest $1,000 for one year, you would earn $80. And if you leave that $80 on deposit the next year, you will earn interest on that amount too. Over time, you can double, even triple, your investment without adding any additional funds of your own.

The "Rule of 72" will tell you how long it will take to double your money. Simply divide 72 by the annual rate of interest. The result is the number of years it will take for your money to double. So at 8 percent interest, your original $1,000 investment would become $2,000 in just 9 years. If you begin as a young adult and leave that money on deposit until retirement at age 67, that $1,000 investment would grow to $36,000. If you were to add an additional $1,000 each year, your fund would total $418,426 at retirement, based on a total investment of only $45,000.

Start planning for your retirement now. It is never too late to begin.

DETERMINE WHOM TO PLAN FOR

After making the decision to get started, you must decide on your goals for retirement planning. First, who will be included in your plan? Your primary goal should be to provide living capital for yourself and your spouse. Aim to meet your own basic needs first. Next, consider your children or others who may be dependent on you. Will your children be independent when your income is reduced by retirement? How will you close the gap between what you have previously earned and what your needs will be?

STEP 9. EDUCATION

For many people, providing a higher education for children is a high priority. This is also one of the biggest challenges in the personal financial journey. College can be quite expensive, and the inflation factor means that costs are constantly rising. Generally, both parents and the student contribute some funding for college. As you begin to plan, remember that there are a large number of funding sources available, such as scholarships, grants, work-study jobs, student loans, Parent Plus loans, educational savings accounts, 529 plans, and savings accounts through institutions like Wesleyan Investment Foundation. Begin early and search broadly for funding options.

It is recommended that you contribute to your retirement savings plan first. Once you are able to make regular consistent contributions to your retirement plan, then you can begin making contributions to your education savings plan. Otherwise if you are married during your retirement years, you may compromise your ability to provide for you and your spouse and will therefore be dependent on your children to provide for you.

SET YOUR RETIREMENT GOALS

Your next step is to determine what you want to accomplish through retirement investing. One way to clarify those goals is to work through this series of questions. Your answers will form the target at which you are aiming.

- When do you hope to retire?
- At retirement, will your wage earning be reduced or eliminated? If reduced, to what level?
- How will your expenses change at retirement?
- What other assets or income sources do you anticipate besides your earnings and investments?
- What will be your income need, adjusted for inflation?
- What is your risk tolerance? That is, how much market volatility are you willing to accept as you invest? *(Typically, this goes down the closer you get to retirement.)*
- How long do you expect to need income after retirement?

Once you have established your retirement goals, you are ready to set an investment strategy.

CREATE AN INVESTMENT STRATEGY

Investing money is not as complicated as some would have you believe. The idea is really quite simple. You set aside a portion of your investing, then choose from a variety of options for investing that money at interest. You don't have to be a stockbroker to invest for your retirement. Just follow these simple steps.

1. Begin with Tax-Deferred Plans. A tax-deferred plan allows you to exempt money from income tax that is invested in certain approved investment plans, such as company pensions or 401Ks. There are many such plans to choose from, but you might begin with the plan offered by your employer, if there is one. As a rule of thumb, invest a minimum of 10 percent of your income in such plans, plus any matching funds that your employer may contribute.

2. Invest Consistently. Dollar cost averaging (DCA) is an investment technique that reduces the impact of volatility. By dividing the total sum to be invested in the market (for example $10,000) into equal amounts over time (say, $100 over 100 weeks), DCA reduces the risk of losing a large amount due to a temporary downturn in the market. Simply put, you are usually better off to invest on a consistent basis over time.

3. Add an Individual Retirement Account (IRA). In addition to your employer plan, consider using an IRA, such as those offered by Wesleyan Investment Foundation. It is wise to diversify your investments a bit, and an IRA gives you a great deal of control over the investment.

4. Invest Conservatively as Retirement Approaches. In earlier years, you may be willing to invest in some funds that promise a higher possible return, but may also be more likely to incur losses. As your time before retirement shortens, switch to less risky funds, which generally produce a lower yield.

It is true that investing can be a bit complex, but the theory behind retirement planning is simple. Consistently invest a portion of your income in pre-tax, interest bearing accounts. Start early, invest consistently, and you'll be ready for retirement when the time comes.

Now that you understand the ABC's of retirement planning and saving for education expenses, there's one more type of financial planning that you'll need to do. This is the last thing you would think of—literally. We'll find out about it in the next chapter.

10
YOU NEED AN ESTATE PLAN!

STEP 10. ESTATE PLANNING

After singer Michael Jackson died on June 25, 2009, there was a fury of controversy surrounding his personal physician that culminated in a guilty verdict for involuntary manslaughter in his treatment of the pop icon. The longer lasting controversy, however, concerned the King of Pop's estate. Executors and family members had been warring over the disposition of Jackson's assets until the executors announced they would fund Michael Jackson's trust with $30 million. Funding is when assets are transferred into a trust. Now money can be distributed to Michael's mother and three children who, along with charity, are the beneficiaries of Michael's trust.

That may not be the end of the story. In a recent year, Forbes named the Jackson estate as number one on its list of top-earning dead celebrities, at $170 million in annual income. The trustees, who are the same two people as the estate executors, continue to decide how and when the money is distributed.

The bickering is likely to continue for some time.[6]

This is why experts advise people to transfer their bank accounts, real estate, and other holdings into a trust during their lifetime—so they, not the executors, can determine how and when the funds are distributed.

Are you confused yet?

While most people—even most celebrities—do not have the wealth of Michael Jackson, nearly everyone has some assets that will remain when they are gone. Whether it is just an old car and a few hundred dollars or thousands, even millions of dollars' worth of assets, every estate has some value. And nearly every estate can become an object of contention if the owner's will is not made perfectly clear.

In other words, you need an estate plan. Do you have questions about estate planning? Let's find some answers.

WHAT IS ESTATE PLANNING?

Estate planning is simply anticipating and arranging for the disposal of your assets during your lifetime—rather than forcing someone else to do it after you are gone. The purpose of estate planning is to eliminate uncertainty and maximize the value of the estate by reducing taxes and other expenses. The specific goals, however, are whatever you would like them to be. An estate plan puts you, not a judge, in control of your assets. In addition to planning for the distribution of assets, an estate plan can designate a guardian for your minor children in the event of your death or incapacitation. An estate plan allows you to designate the use of your assets to provide for your family or other needs in the best possible way.

> **Without a will, you lose control over your property, and the state will appoint a guardian and trustee for your children.**

---

[6]. Danielle and Andy Mayoras, "Pass The Turkey With A Side Of Celebrity Estate Planning Stories," Forbes.com, November 14, 2011, accessed April 20, 2015, http://www.forbes.com/sites/trialandheirs/2011/11/14/what-do-kim-kardashian-and-michael-jackson-have-to-do-with-thanksgiving/

WHAT IS A WILL?

A will (sometimes called a *testament*) is a legal declaration through which a person (*testator*) designates one or more people (*executors*) to manage his or her estate and provides specific instructions for the distribution of assets after the testator's death. A person who dies without a will is called *intestate*. In such cases, state law will determine the distribution of the person's assets. Remarkably, 70 percent of North Americans do not have a will. Of those who do, only about 11 percent leave anything to a church or a charity. A will names the *beneficiaries* of the estate, that is, those who will receive assets, and it states how those assets are to be distributed.

WHY SHOULD I HAVE A WILL?

Virtually everyone should have a will because without one, the state law will determine what happens to your possessions—and your minor children. If you have a will, you decide how your property will be distributed, and you have a say in how your children will be cared for in the event of your death. Without a will, you lose control over your property, and the state will appoint a guardian and trustee for your children.

WHAT OTHER ELEMENTS ARE PART OF ESTATE PLANNING?

There are a number of other legal instruments or terms that may come into estate planning. Here is a brief survey.

Probate is the legal process overseen by a judge that resolves all claims and distributes the deceased person's property under a will. A probate judge decides on the validity of the will and gives approval, also known as granting probate to the executor to administer the estate.

Revocable Living Trust. A trust is an agreement in which funds or property is held by one party for the benefit of another. A will may establish a trust, which, after death, is managed by a trustee. This is a way to leave money for the benefit of minor children, charities, or other purposes without distributing it all at once.

A revocable living trust offers a lot of advantages.

- First, it can avoid many of the legal expenses and delay associated with probate by clarifying the terms of the distribution of an estate.
- A trust also maintains privacy because while a will is a public document, a trust is not.
- A revocable living trust is also highly versatile because it can be modified at any time during the creator's lifetime, including changing beneficiaries, replacing trustees, or even dissolving the trust.

Power of Attorney is a written authorization to conduct legal business on behalf of another person. Power of attorney may be granted for making medical decisions in the event of your incapacitation, or it can be used to grant the right to make financial decisions.

Advanced Directive, also called a *living will,* is an instrument that allows you to declare you intentions regarding your health care in the event of your incapacitation.

DO YOU HAVE AN ESTATE PLAN?

This last question is really the most important. Do you have an estate plan? If not, why not? An estate plan is not expensive to create, and it will save your heirs a great deal of worry, frustration, and possibly even conflict, in the event of your death. An estate plan is the last stop on your roadmap to personal financial stewardship.

Total stewardship begins with you and your personal finances. But it does not end there. In the next section of this book we'll learn the secrets to being a total steward in the next arena where God has granted you resources—your local church.

Part 3

CHURCH FINANCES

Benchmarks for Healthy Churches

Your personal finances are an important part of total stewardship, but God has given you more to manage than your own household. You are also a steward of his Kingdom resources.

Learning to manage the church's funds, property, and assets is the next step in your total stewardship education.

11
THE ABC's OF THE PASTOR'S PAY

If you want to start a tense discussion in a church board meeting, bring up the issue of the pastor's salary. Few topics are as sensitive as the pastor's pay, and there are reasons for that. For one thing, the senior minister's salary, and sometimes that of the staff, is usually a matter of public record. Those who make more than the pastor generally think he or she is paid too little. Members who are paid less tend to see the pastor as overpaid. Some churches even keep the salary intentionally low as a way of exercising control over the pastor. And few understand the complexity of the pastor's compensation package, which, as with any employee, includes expenses for the employer that are not part of the weekly paycheck the pastor receives.

Very few pastors are overpaid, and most work long hours. Certainly no pastor enters the ministry for the money, but it is important for both the minister and the congregation to arrive at a fair level of compensation.

That doesn't have to be as difficult or contentious as it often is. Here are the ABC's of putting together a good compensation plan for a pastor.

HOW TO TALK ABOUT SALARY

The first lesson here is to talk openly, candidly, and frequently about the pastor's compensation. Many pastors are underpaid and feel financial stress that affects their well-being and family. Some of that stress can be reduced by having an annual review of the pastor's salary, initiated by the church board, during which the pastor is free to express his financial need and the church commits to doing an honest review of the pastor's compensation. This goes beyond saying "Let's do the same as last year" to considering all of the factors that go into any employee compensation plan and ensuring that the church treats the pastor fairly.

If your church has not conducted a thorough review of compensation in the last two years, request one.

BASE SALARY AND RELATED ITEMS

Salary. The most basic element of any compensation plan is the salary. This is the gross pay, prior to any deductions for tax, pension, or health care premiums. If unsure what a pastor's base pay should be, consider creating a benchmark by evaluating comparable congregations in your denomination or in your community. Also consider the pastor's level of experience and education.

Housing Allowance. Clergy are eligible to receive a housing allowance, according to U.S. IRS rules, which is not subject to federal income tax. For clergy who live in a parsonage provided by the church, the fair rental value of the property plus any housing related expenses paid by the church is the housing allowance. This amount is subject to self-employment tax but not federal income tax. If the housing allowance is paid in cash, the amount must be designated in writing by the church prior to the start of the year.

Pension. Pension contributions made by the local church are usually based on a percentage of the gross salary including housing allowance. In addition, the pastor may request the deduction of a portion of salary as a voluntary, pre-tax contribution to the pension plan or a tax-sheltered annuity.

HEALTH INSURANCE

Churches that provide a group health plan pay all or a portion of the premium as a benefit of employment. Employer premiums paid directly to the insurance carrier are not taxable. However, money paid directly to the pastor for the purpose of purchasing self-paid health insurance or the employee portion of the group health premium is taxable income.

SELF-EMPLOYMENT TAX

Pastors are considered self-employed by the IRS and must pay self-employment tax. Normally, the employer is required to pay 50 percent of the Social Security tax for employees, and the employee is responsible for the other half. Because pastors are in a unique category—working for the church as their only employer, yet considered self-employed—many churches choose to pay 50 percent of the pastor's self-employment tax, just as they must do for non-clergy employees.

Speaking of taxation, pastors may choose to have taxes deducted from their pay by the church, or they may choose to receive their gross pay in full and make quarterly estimated tax payments to the state and the IRS. The advantage of having taxes deducted by the church is that it is simpler for the pastor. The advantage of making estimated tax payments is that the pastor receives the entire gross pay each pay period and can earn interest on that amount before making the quarterly payments.

SOCIAL SECURITY OPT-OUT

Pastors are offered the one-time choice of opting out of the Social Security system (see IRS Publication 517). By opting out of the system, the pastor gains the flexibility to invest the money that would otherwise be paid to Social Security, possibly securing a more advantageous return. However, this opt-out may be made only on religious grounds (not for purely financial reasons), and the choice may never be reversed. A word of caution is in order. Most pastors that opt out of the Social Security system end up spending the money instead of investing it wisely. This creates a double-whammy during retirement, because the pastor has no Social Security available, and no investments to offset this loss.

VACATION

Vacation time is one of the least-expensive benefits a church can provide for its pastor. Many congregations have unclear policies concerning vacation, study leave, or other paid time off. Your district may have specific guidelines that the church must follow. If there is no clear policy, request that the church establish one. Then make the most of the time allotted.

It is important for both the minister and the congregation to arrive at a fair level of compensation.

Are you unclear about the elements of the pastor's pay? Do you wonder if you are underpaid? Is there some form of compensation that you would like the church to address? Start the conversation. The best way to talk about the pastor's salary is openly, honestly, and frequently, at least once per year.

In the church as in any secular context, employee costs are usually the largest single item in the budget. But there are many other costs to manage as well. It's imperative to get a handle on the budgeting process. Let's tackle that next.

12
CHURCH BUDGETING MADE EASY

Most church members—and many pastors—have a fundamental misunderstanding of the church budget and budget process. They think of the budget as a financial document, and they consider the budget process to be a necessary administrative evil. As a result, many congregations give this vital process little time and attention. Last year's budget is rubber-stamped with nominal increases for inflation, and the budget is placed in a file folder, never to be seen again.

What a mistake!

In fact, the budget is not a purely financial document. It is a blueprint for ministry and a valuable tool for ensuring that effective ministry takes place. The budget process is no mere formality, but a critical step in the management of God's resources. Church budgeting is total stewardship at its best—God's resources applied to the church's vision for Kingdom advancement. This is exciting work.

> *Begin the budget process by asking "What would God have us accomplish next year?"*

If your church board has sloughed through the budget process with little time and attention, these simple steps will help you take control of this incredibly powerful tool for making ministry happen. Let's find out how it works.

1. START WITH A VISION

Budget time is the moment when you put all your ideas on the table, dreaming, praying, seeking what God would have the congregation accomplish in the next year. This is not wild-eyed idealism but sober, prayerful consideration of God's leading. This is your best opportunity to ensure that the actual work of the congregation clearly aligns with the vision the congregation has for ministering to the saints and reaching the lost. Include key stakeholders in this discussion. Talk about it with staff. Gather input from ministry leaders. Review your church's vision and mission. Begin the budget process by asking "What would God have us accomplish next year?"

2. ESTABLISH PRIORITIES

From this vision, establish funding priorities for the coming year. What are the broad areas that you want to target for growth or advancement? This is not line-level budgeting, not yet. This is "top line" thinking. Is it time for a big push in evangelism? Do you want to add staff in a ministry area? Do facility needs have to take center stage? List the few (no more than 3 to 5) major areas where you want to see growth.

3. DETERMINE FUNDING FOR THE COMING YEAR

When you know what you want to accomplish, your next step is to identify funding. Funding may come from a variety of sources (more on that in the next section). The primary source will be tithes and offerings, and current giving will give you a good idea what that will be. However, beware of cutting and pasting last year's offering number. Consider the trajectory of giving. Is it trending up or down? Have you recently gained or lost givers?

Your weekly per-capita giving is a valuable tool for forecasting income. To find your average, divide your average weekly offering by the average number of worship attendees (including children). The national average for weekly per capita giving is $26. If your number is below that, some teaching on stewardship may be in order.

To that number, add other sources of funding. You may gain funding from:

- User fees or registrations.
- Special offerings or pledges.
- Loans.
- Subsidiary ministries, such as a childcare.

Think carefully and include your treasurer or bookkeeper in the discussion. He or she may know of revenue streams that have escaped your notice.

4. SET FINANCIAL BENCHMARKS

Establishing financial benchmarks will keep you from over- or under-spending in key areas. A general guideline is the Rule of Thirds: spend one-third on property, one-third on people, and one-third on programs. You may benefit from knowing some national averages here as well. Experts recommend:

- Spending 30 to 55 percent on salaries.
- Carrying a maximum debt-to-annual offerings ratio of 3:1.

- Having debt payments totaling no more than 33 percent of offerings.
- Earmarking 4 percent of income for capital investment.
- Establishing a reserve fund equal to at least one month's operating expenses.

Most church budgets are zero-based, meaning that income minus expenses for the year equals zero. However, in order to save up reserve funds or pay for unforeseen special projects or needs, budgeting for a surplus is wise.

5. DETERMINE FIXED COSTS

As with your household budget, some expenses are already established and must be paid before discretionary spending can take place. These fixed costs include such things as debt payments, insurance, denominational assessments, utilities, and existing salaries. Budget time is a good time to consider cost reductions. Can you reduce or eliminate any of these costs? Will any go up due to rate increases or inflation?

6. FUND DISCRETIONARY ITEMS

Now it's time to apply your available resources to the mission. Use your established priorities and financial benchmarks as a guide, and allocate your discretionary funding to accomplish your goals. At this stage, staff members and ministry leaders should be asked to supply specific plans for the coming year's ministries, including a projection of how their allocated funds will be spent. This budget becomes both the blueprint for ministry and a tool for accountability.

7. RATIFY THE BUDGET

The church budget is not the creation of any one person, and the entire congregation must own it. Every church has a specific manner for approving the budget. Take that opportunity to communicate the vision for the coming year, and ask the leaders and congregation to support that vision with their affirmation and with their giving.

8. MANAGE THE BUDGET THROUGHOUT THE YEAR

The budget is a blueprint for ministry and a tool for accountability, but only if it is put to use. Don't merely approve the budget then put it in a file. Refer to it when making spending decisions. Request monthly reports that show progress in giving and spending. Ask questions of ministry leaders to find out why they may be over- or under-spending in a particular area. Your church budget is a roadmap to ministry effectiveness. Follow it!

Your church budget is a critical tool for accountability, but you need others. Without them, you could wind up like the church we will read about in the next chapter.

13

ACCOUNTABILITY: YOUR STAY OUT OF JAIL FREE CARD

The former treasurer of a Brookfield, Missouri, church has been sentenced to twenty-one months in prison for embezzling funds from the congregation. According to the FBI, the woman wrote unauthorized church checks to herself and made unauthorized withdrawals from the church's bank account. She also made unauthorized purchases with church checks at local Wal-Mart stores for computers, cameras, and vacuum cleaners only to then return the purchased items for cash. The fraud scheme began in September of 2007 and lasted until October of 2013, and netted approximately $192,000 in fraudulent proceeds. The FBI also noted that, as treasurer, this woman held a position of trust within the congregation, which significantly contributed to the commission and concealment of the fraud.[7]

Sadly, that story is not unique. Incidents like this happen when financial pressure, opportunity, and rationalization combine to form the *Fraud Triangle*. When faced with mounting personal bills, ready access to church funds, and

---

7. *U.S. Attorney's Office*, "Brookfield, Missouri Church Treasurer Sentenced on Fraud Charges," *Federal Bureau of Investigation*, January 14, 2015, accessed April 21, 2015, http://www.fbi.gov/stlouis/press-releases/2015/brookfield-missouri-church-treasurer-sentenced-on-fraud-charges.

the belief that "I'm underpaid" or "They'll never miss it," a pastor, treasurer, or other leader can all too easily succumb to the temptation to misuse church funds. Others fall into illegal or unethical practices through ignorance or carelessness.

Either way, your church needs strong financial controls to ensure that God's resources are used legitimately and that church leaders remain above reproach. Here is a quick-reference list of best practices for establishing financial accountability in your church.

1. Have Multiple Offering Counters. Never allow one person to handle money alone. Ensure that at least two are present when cash or checks are handled.

2. Don't Allow Offering Counters to Deposit Funds. Appoint someone other than the offering counters to take funds to the bank.

3. Have Checks Issued by Two Persons: A Preparer and a Signer. If the person who makes out the check cannot sign it, and vice versa, there is little chance for misuse of checks.

4. Minimize the Use of Signature Stamps. Require hand-written signatures, especially on checks or documents for larger amounts.

5. Audit Monthly Statements. Appoint a neutral person to examine monthly statements to match bank deposits against offering tallies and check for other discrepancies.

6. Use Accounting Software. Electronic records are more accurate and easier to audit.

7. Require Approvals for Spending. All purchases should be reviewed and approved by a third party. This can be done after the fact by reviewing credit statements, signing bills, etc. If the pastor normally approves spending, someone else must be appointed to review the pastor's purchases.

8. Conduct an Annual Audit. The most reliable picture of church funds will be revealed by an external audit conducted by an accountant. This can be expensive, and a congregation may not be able to afford it every year. At a minimum, neutral persons in the congregation should conduct an annual internal audit.

Financial accountability is not difficult to maintain once established. If your church does not have strong financial controls, implement them immediately. You cannot afford to squander the resources you have been given, and you want yourself and each member of your congregation to be guarded against unethical—even illegal—behavior. Strong financial controls are a protection to the church, pastor, staff, and those who handle funds on behalf of the church.

One key for financial accountability in your congregation is timely and accurate reporting on financial matters. Dry and dusty documents that nobody looks at? They need not be. Your financial reports can be some of the most exciting things you read each month. Let's talk about that next.

14

HOW TO CREATE A FINANCIAL DASHBOARD

American Airlines Flight 965 departed Miami International Airport on December 20, 1995, bound for Cali, Colombia. It was a regularly scheduled run, and the pilots and crew were highly experienced at flying the Boeing 757-200 aircraft. Pilots use several radio beacons to approach the Cali airport, nestled high in the mountains. This airplane's flight computer had the beacons' coordinates pre-programmed, which should have told the pilots exactly where to turn, climb, and descend, all the way from Miami to the terminal in Cali. However, since the winds were calm that day, flight controllers asked if the pilots wanted to fly a straight-in approach to runway 19 rather than coming around to runway 01.

The pilots agreed to the shorter route but then mistakenly cleared the approach waypoints from their navigation computer. Attempting to reprogram the coordinates for the waypoint named Rozo, the pilots accidentally selected the preprogrammed coordinates for another waypoint beginning with the letter R, waypoint Romeo, which is near Bogotá. By choosing the wrong coordinates, the pilots placed the aircraft on a collision course with a 9,800-

foot mountain. Seconds later the massive airliner collided with the mountain, killing 159 passengers and eight crewmembers. Only four people survived.

When it comes to navigation, information errors can be deadly. With the right information, you can direct yourself and your vessel anywhere you choose to go. By looking at the wrong information, you place yourself on a course for disaster.

The same is true when it comes to total stewardship of your church. When you have accurate financial information, you can chart a course to any destination. However, if your financial dashboard feeds you the wrong numbers, it could lead to financial ruin.

What are the numbers you should review to ensure financial health? Who is responsible for gathering that information? When? How? Let's look at the steps to creating an accurate financial dashboard for your church.

1. SELECT YOUR DASHBOARD INSTRUMENTS

The information you choose to gather will determine the soundness of your financial decision making. There is no single set of reliable indicators, but you may wish to choose from these commonly used reporting tools.

Average Weekly Offerings. Review this number monthly, and examine trending versus previous months and previous years.

Weekly Per-Capita Giving. This is the average weekly offering amount divided by the average weekly attendance, including children. This is a good indication of the financial strength and commitment of the congregation. The national average is about $26.

Income Statement. This shows total income, including tithes and offerings, designated gifts, and revenue from other sources. It should compare the income to the previous month and the same period in the last year.

Budget Variance Report. This report compares the line-level budget to actual income and spending for any period, usually the current month and the year-to-date. This vital indicator is your early warning system to reveal potential financial problems.

Balance Sheet. This document shows the overall financial position of the church, including all assets and liabilities. This includes more than just cash on hand. Assets include real estate, stocks and other investments, outstanding receivables, and all cash accounts. Liabilities include debts, designated funds, and outstanding payables (including loans).

Number of New Givers. This indicates whether or not newcomers are fully committing to the mission of the church.

Number of Consistent Givers. Because people often give intermittently based on their income, you'll have to determine what "consistent" means. At least one significant gift per quarter might qualify. This tracks the overall number of people supporting the church's mission.

Number of Givers to Special Appeals. This includes missions giving, special offerings, and capital campaigns. The higher the ratio of special givers to total givers is; the stronger the financial strength of the church is.

> **The information you choose to gather will determine the soundness of your financial decision making.**

2. SELECT THE FREQUENCY OF REPORTING

Most financial reports are generated monthly. Certainly, the income statement and budget variance report should be reviewed at least that often. A more thorough look at the financial dashboard might be done quarterly. Some items would be reviewed annually in connection with budgeting and stewardship planning.

3. ASSIGN REPORTING DUTIES

Some of the financial data will be gathered and reported by the treasurer, of course. The pastor and the chairperson of the finance committee should also play a role in evaluating the financial data for use in decision making. Assign the roles and tasks of your financial reporting structure.

4. REPORT TO THE PROPER ENTITIES

Some leaders have a tendency to hoard financial data believing that others would make rash decisions if they had "all the facts." Nothing could be further from the truth. Pastors, church boards, finance committees, and the congregation as a whole cannot make sound ministry decisions without an accurate picture of the church's financial health. Reports are typically made to the following entities.

Pastor. The pastor should review all financial reports. Some pastors choose to receive donor reports as well as church-wide financial reports so that they know the giving patterns of individual members.

Church Board. The board should have access to all church-wide financial data, but the volume can be overwhelming. From your dashboard, choose which reports to provide to the board on a monthly basis and which to provide less often. Because these reports can be somewhat technical, the treasurer or finance committee chair should interpret them for the board.

Donors. Congregations should provide a record of donor contributions to each individual at least annually. Many churches report this quarterly as a way of better communicating the church's financial aims and needs with members.

Congregation. The congregation should be informed of the church's financial position at least annually. The budget report and balance sheet should be included.

Denomination. Your district and denomination also need to know your congregation's financial position. Report to them according to the schedule they require. And always share significant financial news, whether good or bad, with your superintendent.

Good decisions begin with good information. Disastrous decisions often result from faulty or missing information. Create a solid financial dashboard, and use it consistently to place your church on firm financial ground.

There is one more thing you need to know about handling your church's finances, and that is the proper way to handle designated contributions. Let's see if you have made any of the common mistakes listed in the next chapter.

15

THE SIX MOST COMMON MISTAKES IN HANDLING CHARITABLE GIFTS

When you ask people to donate to a special cause, you never quite know what will happen. It's likely that the folks who created Kickstarter, the online funding platform, never anticipated that Zach Danger Brown would use it to raise over $55,000 to make a potato salad. Yes, a potato salad.

Clearly, not every fundraising appeal turns out as intended. Churches, too, can wind up in a place they never expected when accepting charitable gifts.

In August 2014, 6,911 people donated their hard earned cash to help Zach make his first-ever batch of potato salad. His original funding goal was just $10, but this fellow with the middle name, "Danger," became a celebrity of sorts and even appeared on *Good Morning America*. Zach pledged to use the excess funds to host a festival in Columbus, Ohio, that would raise funds to help the homeless.

Clearly, not every fundraising appeal turns out as intended. Churches, too, can wind up in a place they never expected when accepting charitable gifts. Government regulations dictate certain aspects of handling charitable giving, and unwary congregations fall into a few common errors. See if you have ever made one of these common funding mistakes.

MISTAKE 1:
ALLOWING DESIGNATED GIFTS TO DRIVE MINISTRY

"Pastor, I think the church should have a coffee bar in the foyer, and I'm donating $2,500 to install it." Maybe you have heard some version of that line before. Donors often wish to see the church take on a ministry or project and will try to force its approval by giving the funds. Beware of accepting gifts with strings attached. Offer to redirect the giving to one of your existing ministries or goals, but do not allow a giver to make decisions that should be made by church leaders.

MISTAKE 2:
ISSUING CASH RECEIPTS FOR GIFTS IN KIND

"I'd like to donate my old couch for the church youth room. It's worth at least $200. Can you give me a receipt for that amount?" The answer is no. Issue a receipt that lists the goods only (i.e., one used couch). It is up to the donor to substantiate the value of that gift to the IRS. (See the Appendix for a sample receipt.)

MISTAKE 3:
ISSUING TAX-DEDUCTIBLE RECEIPTS WHEN GOODS ARE EXCHANGED

"Buy a calendar to support the youth group for $10. It's tax deductible!" Well, part of it may be. When any goods or premiums are offered for a gift, the fair value of those goods must be subtracted from the receipted value of the donation. So the receipt for the calendar might be $5 rather than $10, depending on the value of the calendar. (See the Appendix for a sample receipt.)

MISTAKE 4:
ALLOWING DONORS TO DIRECT GIFTS FOR INDIVIDUAL USE

"My daughter will be attending a Christian college this fall. I'd like to give $100 to the church scholarship fund and have it designated for her." Nope. Scholarships and other types of special giving may not be directed for the specific use of an individual.

MISTAKE 5:
REDIRECTING DESIGNATED FUNDS

"Pastor, we're behind on our mortgage, but there's $4,000 in the memorial fund. Can't we use that money to catch up?" In a word, "No." Funds accepted for a specific use generally may not be redirected for another purpose. Though specific scenarios are too varied to discuss here, the permission of each donor would be required.

MISTAKE 6:
NOT SAYING THANK YOU

When you are concerned about the mortgage, the bills, missions support, and replacing the church roof you may be too caught up in the struggle to remember what your mom taught you: Say thank you when someone offers a gift. Every dollar you receive represents a sacrifice for the giver. It is important to issue a receipt, but that is not enough. Say "thank you" in your communications, in your offering talks, and in person when appropriate. Let your givers know that their work is truly appreciated.

Avoiding these simple mistakes will ensure that you properly handle charitable gifts. But what happens when you need more funding than what comes through the offering plate? Would you like to add a few dollars to your ministry funding? In the next section, we will learn how to do exactly that.

Part 4

FUND DEVELOPMENT

What Could You Do With More Money?

All leaders have more vision than resources. We could all accomplish greater things if we had more money, more volunteers, more time. In short, we could do more with more resources.

God has promised to supply all of our needs. It is his Kingdom, after all. Yet there are important things we must do to receive and steward those additional funds. In this section, we will learn how total stewardship applies not just to the money you already have but also to the money you hope to receive.

16

HOW TO CREATE NEW GIVERS

A church without problems has either been closed or raptured. But all of the problems aren't about music styles or carpet colors. Money problems can choke the very life out of a congregation. The "giving gap" is one the church's greatest challenges. There are times when you could drive two armored vehicles side-by-side through that gap without waking a parishioner!

There are at least eight ways to close the giving gap.

1. HAVE AN ANNUAL STEWARDSHIP EMPHASIS

Many postmodern congregations do not have a handle on the importance of giving. They are products of a society that thinks it is more blessed to "receive" than to "give." Put the stewardship campaign on the calendar, with as much excitement as a Christmas program. Continually and consistently teach the duties (and delights) of giving.

2. OPEN THE BOOKS

The media focuses on the misgivings and misappropriations of the corporate world. Congregants have developed an "audit mentality." Financial openness that includes regular reporting is crucial to gaining and keeping faithful givers.

3. DEVELOP YOUR BASE

The migration to megachurches has left some mid-size and smaller churches with a reduced giving base. A new generation of givers must be raised up. Start the stewardship training in the kindergarten class instead of in the "senior saints" class. Develop the giving base early. Invite new people into the giving pool. Many people simply need that first opportunity to give.

4. HONOR THE COMMITTED

Many give for recognition rather than inspiration. Teach the cycle of giving—that giving is its own reward. Honor the stewardship commitments of your parishioners. Award their years of service or use their sacrificial efforts as examples in your sermon illustrations, while keeping giving amounts confidential.

5. SET GIVING GOALS

An organization that doesn't focus on the future is stuck with the present "tense." Setting giving goals for God-inspired, congregation-approved projects—and celebrating the victory milestones—will motivate churches of any size.

6. USE GIVING MODELS

What is the gold standard for giving? Your church needs an example as well as an exposition. Use biblical models in your teaching and preaching: Nehemiah's renovation project, the Savior's sacrifice, the widow's mite commitment, the Macedonian church's sacrifice, or the Apostle Paul's compassionate ministries fund.

7. TEACH ABOUT MONEY

People live in a consumer driven society that is often motivated by greed or gain. They have been taught that their money is simply that: "their" money. That is far removed from biblical teaching however: "The earth is the LORD's, and everything in it, the world, and all who live in it" (Ps. 24:1). We preach a stewardship series to emphasize the eternal benefits of giving over the temporal benefits of gaining. By teaching people to manage their lives by managing its individual components (including finances), we have taught them how to be victors instead of victims of their times.

We have a spiritual obligation to protect the flock from the wolves of worldliness—to free their mind, their spirit from the chains of secular materialism. Stephen Wilson pastors a congregation of nearly 2,000 in Greeley, Colorado. He says he preaches an annual stewardship series because, "It is one aspect of a person's faith that most obviously expresses their trust in God." He adds that he doesn't want people to miss out on the blessings that are a part of it.

Offering times should be a highlight of worship, a celebration of what God is doing and will do among us.

---

8. CELEBRATE GIVING AS WORSHIP

In many churches, the offering time is one of the most interesting moments in the worship service. In some churches, it is a time to share casserole recipes in loud whispers. In others, it is a time when the board chairman's granddaughter can sing with her new accompaniment tape. In some churches, offering time is as thrilling as trying on gloves; while in others, it is an exciting time of praise for God's blessings. Offering times should be a highlight of worship, a celebration of what God is doing and will do among us.

You don't have to sing the "bottom line blues." With some Spirit-led planning, you can lead your flock to the higher ground of godly giving.

Creating more givers is one way to increase ministry funding. But there is another way that you need to know about. We will find out what that is in the next chapter.

17
THE MOST COMMON MISTAKE IN CAPITAL FUND DRIVES

A Texas oil tycoon went to a little bank to cash a personal check. The teller returned, "I'm sorry sir, we can't cash this."

"What's the problem?" the surprised oilman asked.

The clerk replied, "Insufficient funds, Sir."

"That can't be!" the man bellowed. "I have plenty of money!"

"Oh no, Sir," the clerk responded. "Not you. It's us!"

God's "bank" is never at risk. His returns are compounded from a bountiful supply. In reality, the problem with funding God's mission is on our side. It is we who believe we have insufficient funds to accomplish all God would have us do.

A capital fund drive is a way of reaching deeper into God's pockets (and ours), connecting the resources God has already provided to the congregation with the mission and ministries of the church. However, there is one colossal mistake that congregations make regarding capital fund drives—they don't have them.

Ignoring this important avenue for gathering God's resources is one of the biggest errors a church can make. God has already given us enough resources to supply nearly every need. Capital funding is a way of unlocking those resources. Here are some of the reasons every church should consider a capital campaign.

Capital funding is merely a way of funding important initiatives that go beyond "offering plate" giving.

EVERY CHURCH HAS CAPITAL NEEDS

We think of capital campaigns primarily as a tool for funding new construction, and that is an important use. However, every congregation has a variety of other needs for capital funding, such as debt retirement, infrastructure upgrades, major maintenance, and launching new ministries. Capital funding is merely a way of funding important initiatives that go beyond "offering plate" giving.

PROPERTY EXPENSES CAN OVERWHELM A CONGREGATION

Most churches run on a tight budget, so there is often little or nothing put away for a rainy day. Even a moderate reserve fund can easily be outstripped by the staggering cost of a major capital repair—such as adding a new roof, repaving a parking lot, or replacing HVAC equipment.

GROWING CHURCHES NEED MORE ROOM

New and growing congregations need a place to meet, so funding new construction is one use for a capital campaign. There are others that relate to meeting space. Major remodeling, technical equipment upgrades, new furnishings, or repurposing building space are all costly and difficult to do within an annual budget cycle. Additional funds may be needed.

PROPERTIES MUST BE FITTED FOR SPECIAL NEEDS OF ATTENDEES

Accessibility, safety and security, child protection—these are major concerns for our people and should be a major concern for church leaders. Fitting a building for special needs may require special funding.

DEBT MUST BE RETIRED

The capital campaign that funded an original construction project may have left the congregation short of its true need. A high mortgage is an impediment to ministry funding, and old debt must be retired before new projects can be considered.

PASTORAL STAFF CANNOT DO EVERYTHING

We rightly expect our pastors to be experts in teaching the Word, winning souls, and shepherding the flock. It is unreasonable to expect that all pastors will also be experts in fundraising. A capital campaign team can be a great help in assisting a church and its leaders to achieve the vision God has given them.

If you have a vision or pressing need that is significantly larger than your current funding will allow, you need to consider a capital campaign. The money is already in the pews. A good campaign will release those funds for ministry.

Not sure how to go about holding a capital fund drive? The next chapter will show you how.

18

TWELVE STEPS TO A SUCCESSFUL CAMPAIGN

When it comes to raising funds, pastors have taken some creative approaches in the past, not all of them good. Perhaps you heard about the pastor who kicked off a capital campaign for worship center renovations. When it came time for members to pledge, he stood before the congregation and said, "I would like to remind you that what you are about to give is tax deductible, cannot be taken with you, and to love it is considered the root of all evil."

Then there was the pastor who announced the capital campaign for construction of a new building. He told the congregation, "I have good news and bad news. The good news is that we have enough money to pay for our new building program. The bad news is that it's still out there in your pockets." Even that was better than the pastor who distributed bumper stickers to his members that read, "Tithe if you love Jesus. Any fool can honk."

Most of us readily admit that we are not experts at raising money, so the idea of launching a capital campaign can be daunting. Even when we are convinced of the need, we wonder *how* we will ever raise the funds. But capital funding is no great mystery. There are proven steps to holding a successful campaign. With some prayer, planning, and teamwork, you can succeed in funding your vision. Follow these simple steps.

1. CREATE A LONG-TERM STRATEGIC PLAN

Money flows to vision. When people see the long-range big picture that you aim to accomplish, they will be inspired to give. When they see only a broken-down furnace with no strategy for future mission and ministry, they will shy away. Determine your long-term objectives.

2. DETERMINE THE GIVING CAPACITY OF THE CONGREGATION

To estimate the giving capacity of your congregation, you will need the following information.

- Giving history of the church for the last three years.
- Number and distribution of household givers. (That is the total number of givers along with the giving level of each household.)
- Average household income of your community. Check with your local chamber of commerce or Census.gov to determine this amount.

One formula for calculating the giving potential of the congregation is to multiply the number of givers by the average household income, then multiply by 10 percent.

(Total Givers) x (Average Household Income) x (10 percent)

Another rule of thumb is that a campaign will raise between one and three times your church's general fund giving. For small projects, a one-time special offering should yield an amount equal to one regular Sunday offering. This will help you determine what's possible.

3. DETERMINE THE FUNDING NEED

This is a step at which you may need outside consulting, particularly if there is construction involved. An architect, design/build consultant, or technical experts in your project area can help you determine both the best project parameters to meet your goals and the cost of the project. Beware of trying to "guestimate" the cost. Get a clear picture of the total expense.

It costs money to raise money.

4. SET A GOAL FOR THE CAMPAIGN

With a clear picture of both the giving potential of the congregation and the costs of the project you hope to accomplish, you are in a position to set a goal for the campaign. This is a point at which you may need to expand or contract your project outcomes based on potential funding versus estimated cost. Choose a bold but achievable goal, one that will inspire members to take part.

5. SELECT A LEADERSHIP TEAM

The pastor must be the spokesperson for vision, but others are needed to carry the administrative burden of the campaign. Involving others also broadens ownership of the initiative. Select this team including both appointed leaders (such as board members) and informal leaders within the congregation. Appoint a campaign chairperson other than the pastor.

6. DEVELOP A CAMPAIGN PLAN AND BUDGET, AND SEEK APPROVAL

It costs money to raise money. If you work with a funding consultant, determine their fees. If you choose to develop your own campaign, create a plan and budget with line-level detail. Your timeline must be specific also. Consider the timing carefully, and allow for these phases of the campaign.

1. Campaign planning and approvals (3–6 months)
2. Leadership campaign (4–6 weeks)
3. General campaign (4–6 weeks)
4. Pledge Celebration (1 day)
5. Follow-Up Campaign (1 month)
6. Funding (1–3 years)

Seek approval for the plan from the church board or congregation. This must be a team effort.

7. DEVELOP A COMMUNICATIONS STRATEGY

Money flows to vision, and people will give only when they are given the respect of good information and a respectful invitation. It is difficult to over-communicate during a capital campaign. Develop a communication strategy that will achieve these goals, then work that strategy consistently. Your aim should be to communicate these items so that every potential giver is aware of them.

- *What* the project aims to accomplish.
- *Why* this project is necessary.
- *How* the project connects to vision.
- *Where* in Scripture we see that this vision intersects with God's mission.
- *Who* benefits from the work (children, youth, families, the unsaved, etc.).
- *When* the project will take place (timeline for funding, timeline for action).

When you think you have thoroughly communicated these details to every potential giver, congratulations—you're just getting started! Communicate regularly throughout the life of the campaign.

8. CONDUCT A LEADERSHIP CAMPAIGN

To be successful, the general campaign must be strongly supported by the leaders of the church. List the leaders of the congregation—official and unofficial—and ask for their pledge to the campaign. If your vision casting and approvals process have been successful so far, this portion of the campaign will garner strong support and kick-start the wider campaign.

During this phase, also include the top 10 percent of givers to your general fund, whether they hold a leadership position in the congregation or not. Their giving level indicates their support for the church and its vision. These are the givers who have the potential to make a significant contribution. It is not unusual for a single high-capacity giver to pledge 10 percent of the total goal, or more.

This phase of the campaign should be conducted in face-to-face meetings with leaders and high-capacity donors. During these meetings the pastor presents the vision behind the campaign followed by a direct appeal for a pledge. The direct appeal may be made by the pastor or by a member of the campaign committee.

9. CONDUCT THE GENERAL CAMPAIGN

This is the public portion of the campaign during which you intensively communicate the vision, goals, and campaign timeline. Remember to include all constituents of the congregation, not just current contributors. This is a major undertaking of the church; children and teens should be included. Some friends of the church—former attendees, extended family, etc.—will also want to participate. Include them in mailings and other communications. Your general campaign will culminate with a pledge celebration.

10. HOLD A PLEDGE CELEBRATION

Choose a day to make a large-scale event during which the congregation makes their pledge for the campaign. This could be a banquet, a festival-type event, or a Sunday worship service. Giving is an act of worship, and it is totally appropriate to hold this event on Sunday morning. Invite donors to make their pledge, and don't be afraid to inject creativity into the day.

11. CELEBRATE AND GIVE THANKS

At the first opportunity, celebrate the achievement by announcing the total amount pledged. Give thanks first to the Lord, who provides the funds, and also to the generous donors. Each donor should receive a pledge statement as a reminder of his or her faith commitment. A handwritten thank-you note or letter is also a great idea.

12. FOLLOW-UP ON THE CAMPAIGN

A campaign does not end with the pledge celebration. In some ways, it is just beginning. Donors should be encouraged to fulfill their pledges over the next one to three years. Ensure that the campaign is successful by following up in these ways.

- Communicate the progress of the fund every month.
- Send quarterly statements to donors showing their progress on their pledge.
- Communicate the timeline for completion of the project, construction, or purchase funded by the campaign.
- Celebrate completion of the work.
- Invite newcomers and especially new givers to join the campaign.

Follow these steps and you will discover that one of those imaginative preachers mentioned above was actually correct—the money is already there. God has provided the funding we need. We must offer people a compelling reason to give it and provide a clear avenue for doing so. That is the simple idea behind a capital campaign.

Even when your campaign is successful, however, you may need additional funding. To get it, you may need to learn a new language. In the next chapter, you will find out how to talk with a banker.

19

HOW TO TALK TO A BANKER: WHAT YOU NEED TO SECURE A LOAN

A woman walked into a charity second-hand bookstore where all the stock comes from donations. She approached a clerk and asked, "Excuse me, do you have *The Book Thief*?" Fiction shelves are arranged alphabetically by author, so the clerk quickly scanned the stock and reported that there was no copy in stock.

"Oh, no!" the woman said, "I need a used copy. I borrowed one from a friend and she wants it back. But my husband accidentally gave it to a charity shop and he can't remember which one." Wanting to be helpful, the clerk offered to check the backroom, where recent donations were being sorted. A moment later she came back with a copy.

"Thank you so much!" the woman exclaimed. "This may even be the same copy we donated." And she turned to leave the store.

"Great," said the clerk. "That'll be ten dollars."

The woman was stunned. "But I told you," she said, "It was only borrowed." Perhaps she didn't get the irony of the title, *The Book Thief*.

That story illustrates the fundamental principle of borrowing money, and one that many forget—you have to pay it back! When borrowing money, it is vital that you understand a few things about lending, including a few financial terms. Here is what you need to know before talking with a lender.

GENERAL GUIDELINES FOR SECURING A LOAN

- The loan should not be more than three times the church's annual giving from tithes and offerings.
- A lower loan-to-offering ratio is more manageable.
- The borrowed amount should not exceed 75 percent of the project.
- Your capital campaign or other funding should contribute a minimum of 25 percent of the cost.
- The annual debt service should not exceed 30 percent of annual giving from tithes and offerings.
- Understand that not all lenders understand or are sympathetic to churches and church related organizations.

Working with an organization such as Wesleyan Investment Foundation, which exists specifically to assist churches, is an advantage. Also, not all loan proposals are the same as it relates to fees, covenants, or restrictions. The lender will look carefully at all of these things, and you should too.

ITEMS NEEDED FOR A LOAN APPLICATION

Few documents are as complex as the financial instruments used to lend and receive funds. To navigate the loan application process, you will need specific information. Here is a list of the commonly needed items when applying for a loan.

- Financial statements showing income and expenses for the past three years.
- A current year budget showing income and expenses.
- Evidence of local church approval of the loan (i.e., meeting minutes or resolution).
- Evidence of district or other governing body approval of the loan and certification of their willingness to co-sign or guarantee the loan if necessary (i.e., meeting minutes or letter).
- A detailed project budget.
- A signed purchase agreement or contract.
- A detailed statement that includes (1) the justification or need for the loan, (2) photographs of any property, buildings, or other items to be funded by the loan, and (3) a statement of how the loan will be repaid.
- A survey and/or appraisal of the property, if one exists (this may be requested by the lender).

There is no mystery about dealing with a lender. With some homework and a bit of planning, you'll be ready to negotiate your loan like a pro. You may not need to borrow, however. There are still six types of funding that you may be leaving on the table. Let's find out what they are.

20

SIX TYPES OF MONEY YOU'RE LEAVING ON THE TABLE

When people begin to think about the end of their lives, their true feelings may be seen for the first time. Sometimes the results are hilarious. Consider the case of Anthony Scott, who wrote in his last will and testament: "To my first wife Sue, whom I always promised to mention in my will. Hello Sue!" German poet Heinrich Heine left his entire fortune to his wife, but with the proviso that she had to remarry. Why? Because, the poet said, "Then there will be at least one man to regret my death."

Others make bequests with strings attached. In Henry Budd's will in 1862, he left £200,000 in a trust for his two sons on the condition that neither grow a moustache. The last will of a woman named Rosaleen declared, "I give to Stonyhurst Jesuits the sum of £500 for the purchase of thermal underwear."

Some folk, however, are truly generous with their last gift. Pharmaceutical heiress Ruth Lilly was an aspiring poet and spent much of her life trying to get published. Although she was unsuccessful, she did once receive a handwritten rejection letter from the editor of *Poetry* magazine. Based on that slight encouragement, the heiress pledged $100 million worth of stock to the foundation that publishes the journal.

And that brings us to the "last" source of funding for your congregation—planned giving. Incredibly, 70 percent of North Americans do not have a will. That means the laws of the state they last lived in, not they or their family, will decide what becomes of their assets. Of those who have a will, only about 11 percent designate a gift to their local church. If you are not encouraging members to create an estate plan, you are leaving untold amounts of money on the table—money that could be used for God's kingdom.

> **Incredibly, 70 percent of North Americans do not have a will.**

SIX TYPES OF PLANNED GIVING

Not every planned gift comes after the donor has deceased, however. You should be aware of these six types of planned giving.

1. Wills or Bequests. A will (sometimes called a *testament*) is a legal declaration through which a person (*testator*) designates one or more people (*executors*) to manage his or her estate and provides it specific instructions for the distribution of the estate after the testator's death.

2. Charitable Gift Annuity. A gift annuity is a contract between a donor and a charity through which the donor transfers cash or property to the charity in exchange for a partial tax deduction and a lifetime stream of annual income from the charity. When the donor dies, the charity keeps the gift.

3. Charitable Trust. A charitable trust is an irrevocable trust established for charitable purposes. The trust may be established during the donor's lifetime for the benefit of a charitable organization. A trust is controlled by trustees.

4. Endowment Fund. An endowment fund is established by an institution and contributed to by donors. The donations are tax deductible for the donors, and the institution withdraws funds at regular intervals for the fund's specified purpose.

5. *Memorial Fund.* A memorial fund is a fund established in memory of an individual. It may be established by the institution or by a donor. Tax-deductible contributions are made by donors and used by the institution for the fund's stated purpose.

6. *Donor Advised Fund.* A donor advised fund is a charitable fund administered by a public charity but created to manage charitable donations on behalf of an organization, family, or individual. To participate in a donor advised fund, a donating individual or organization opens an account in the fund and deposits cash, securities, or other financial instruments. Donors surrender ownership of anything they put in the fund but retain control over how their account is invested, and how its proceeds are distributed to charities.

ADVANTAGES OF PLANNED GIVING

Planned giving can benefit the church as the recipient of gifts. There are significant benefits for the donor as well. It serves the interests of both the church and parishioners to engage in estate planning. By giving through a will or bequest, the donor minimizes estate tax liability and minimizes probate, which may significantly speed the distribution of assets. Giving of this type is best done as a percentage of the total estate.

A gift annuity offers donors a way to further the causes they believe in while possibly benefitting from one or more of the following:

- Lifetime payments to the donor that may be partially tax-free or taxed at rates lower than regular income.
- Professional management of assets.
- Immediate increase in income to the donor.
- A charitable tax-deduction in the year of the gift.
- Estate tax savings.
- Reduced capital gains taxes.

Consider offering an estate-planning workshop in connection with your annual stewardship teaching. If members are not considering ways to distribute the wealth they leave behind, they are not practicing total stewardship. Help them with this aspect of stewardship, and both the church and the members will be blessed.

AFTERWORD

What would be possible for you and your family if finances were not a problem? What could you and your congregation accomplish with unlimited resources? The good news is that God holds all the wealth that there is, and he has given it to us to manage on his behalf. Jesus fed the five thousand and turned jars of water into fine wine for a joyous celebration. And he promised, "Very truly I tell you, whoever believes in me will do the works I have been doing, and they will do even greater things than these, because I am going to the Father" (John 14:12). The question is not "Do we have the resources?" God has all the resources that there are and provides them for our use. The real question is "Will we carefully tend and boldly use the resources that he has already provided?"

Total stewardship is a completely new way of understanding stewardship. It begins with a lifestyle of abundance, generosity, and openness to others, and it leads to our open-handed management of all that God has given to us. When we recognize two foundational truths, everything else falls into line.

Truth One: God has blessed us abundantly with all that we need in this world.

Truth Two: God invites us to join him in tending to the good world he created.

Are you ready for a life of total stewardship? Are you willing to be the vessel through which God's abundance can flow? Let's take this journey together. Only heaven knows what we can accomplish together.

APPENDIX

Sample gift receipt for gift in kind.

Any Town Church
Any Drive
Any Town, Any State

Mr. John Q. Donor
Any Street
Any Town, Any State

Dear Mr. Donor:

Thank you so much for volunteer services you provided to Any Town Church during 2014. Your efforts in serving as a Commercial Electrician (describe volunteer position) have contributed to the accomplishment of our mission.

While federal tax law does not permit volunteers to deduct the value of their personal services as charitable contributions, volunteers are permitted to deduct out-of-pocket expenses they incur in providing such services. For example, if you purchased and donated materials in connection with your volunteer services, you may deduct those expenses. Other examples included your out-of-pocket expenses for travel, lodging, etc. in connection with providing services. Federal law also permits volunteers who use their vehicles in providing services to charities to deduct their mileage costs at a standard rate of 14 cents per mile. Of course, the expenses described in this paragraph are only deductible if the volunteers are not reimbursed for them.

In order to deduct the expenses described above, you must have a proper documentation to support the amounts deducted. You may find IRS Publication 526, "Charitable Contributions" helpful in this regard. We can provide a copy of Publication 526 upon request. You should consult your tax advisor to determine the amount, if any, you may actually deduct on your tax return.

This letter will serve to confirm that we provided you with no goods or services in exchange for your contribution of services described herein, or related out-of-pocket expenses you may have incurred.

Thank you again for your generous service.

Sincerely,

Mary Q. Bookkeeper

Treasurer

Sample gift receipt for exchange of value.

Any Town Church
Any Drive
Any Town, Any State

Any Town Church
Any Drive
Any Town, Any State

Dear Mr. Donor:

Thank you so much for purchasing the Any Town Church calendar. This letter will serve as a formal acknowledgement for federal tax purposes that you made a gift of $10.00 on 01/02/15. You received goods and services in exchange for the gift valued at $2.00. [See below] Federal tax law permits you to deduct as a charitable contribution on the excess (if any) of your gift over the value of items you received in exchange. Thank you for your support.

Sincerely,

Mary Q. Bookkeeper

Treasurer

[A description of the goods and services should be included. In this example the item was stated in the first line.]

Notes

Notes

Notes

Notes

Notes

Notes

Notes

Notes

Notes

Notes

Notes

Notes

Notes